William

Arthur Clutton-Brock

Author: Arthur Clutton-Brock

Layout: Baseline Co. Ltd.
127-129A Nguyen Hue Blvd
Fiditourist, 3rd floor
District 1, Ho Chi Minh City
Vietnam

© 2007, Confidential Concepts, worldwide, USA
© 2007, Parkstone Press International, New York, USA

Published in 2007 by Grange Books
an imprint of Grange Books Plc
The Grange Kingsnorth Industrial Estate
Hoo, nr Rochester, Kent ME3 9ND
www.grangebooks.co.uk

ISBN: 978-1-84013-887-0

Printed in China

Editor's Note
Out of respect to the author's original work, this text has not been corrected or
updated, particularly regarding attribution, dates, and the current locations of
works. These were uncertain at the time of the text's first publication, and
sometimes remain so to this day. The information in the captions, however,
has been updated.

William
Morris

Arthur Clutton-Brock

Contents

WILLIAM·MORRIS

Introduction

From the middle of the nineteenth century to the beginning of the twentieth century, we have passed through a period of aesthetic discontent which continues and which is distinct from the many kinds of discontent by which men have been troubled in former ages. No doubt aesthetic discontent has existed before; men have often complained that the art of their own time was inferior to the art of the past; but they have never before been so conscious of this inferiority or felt that it was a reproach to their civilisation and a symptom of some disease affecting the whole of their society. We, powerful in many things beyond any past generation of men, feel that in this one respect we are more impotent than many tribes of savages. We can make things such as men have never made before; but we cannot express any feelings of our own in the making of them, and the vast new world of cities which we have made and are making so rapidly, seems to us, compared with the little slow-built cities of the past, either blankly inexpressive or pompously expressive of something which we would rather not have expressed. That is what we mean when we complain of the ugliness of most modern things made by men. They say nothing to us or they say what we do not want to hear, and therefore we should prefer a world without them.

For us there is a violent contrast between the beauty of nature and the ugliness of man's work which most past ages have felt little or not at all. We think of a town as spoiling the country, and even of a single modern house as a blot on the face of the earth. But in the past, until the eighteenth century, men thought that their own handiwork heightened the beauty of nature or was, at least, in perfect harmony with it. We are aware of this harmony in a village church or an old manor house or a thatched cottage, however plain these may be; and wonder at it as a secret that we have lost.

Indeed, it is a secret definitely lost in a period of about forty years, between 1790 and 1830. In the middle of the eighteenth century, foolish furniture, not meant for use, was made for the rich, both in France and in England; furniture meant to be used was simple, well made, and well proportioned. Palaces might have been pompous and irrational, but plain houses still possessed the merits of plain furniture. Indeed, whatever men made, without trying to be artistic, they made well; and their work had a quiet unconscious beauty, which passed unnoticed until the secret of it was lost. When the catastrophe came, it affected less those arts such as painting, which are supported by the conscious patronage of the rich, than those more universal and necessary arts which are maintained by a general and unconscious liking for good workmanship and rational design. There were still painters like Turner and Constable, but soon neither rich nor poor could buy new furniture or any kind of domestic implement that was not hideous. Every new building was vulgar or mean, or both.

1. **Cosmo Rowe**, *Portrait of William Morris*, c. 1895.
Oil on canvas.
Wightwick Manor, Staffordshire.

Everywhere the ugliness of irrelevant ornament was combined with the meanness of grudged material and bad workmanship.

At the time no one seems to have noticed this change. None of the great poets of the Romantic Movement, except perhaps Blake, gives a hint of it. They turned with an unconscious disgust from the works of man to nature; and if they speak of art at all it is the art of the Middle Ages, which they enjoyed because it belonged to the past. Indeed the Romantic Movement, so far as it affected the arts at all, only afflicted them with a new disease. The Gothic revival, which was a part of the Romantic movement, expressed nothing but a vague dislike of the present with all its associations and a vague desire to conjure up the associations of the past as they were conjured up in Romantic poetry. Pinnacles, pointed arches and stained glass windows were symbols, like that blessed word Mesopotamia; and they were used without propriety or understanding. In fact, the revival meant nothing except that the public was sick of the native ugliness of its own time and wished to make an excursion into the past, as if for change of air and scene.

But this weariness was at first quite unconscious. Men were not aware that the art of their time was afflicted with a disease, still less had they any notion that that disease was social. They had lost a joy in life, but they did not know it until Ruskin came to tell them that they had lost it and why. In him æsthetic discontent first became conscious and scientific. For he saw that the prevailing ugliness was not caused merely by the loss of one particular faculty, that the artistic powers of men were not isolated from all their other powers. He was the first to judge works of art as if they were human actions, having moral and intellectual qualities as well as æsthetic; and he saw their total effect as the result of all those qualities and of the condition of the society in which they were produced. So his criticism gave a new importance to works of art, as being the clearest expression of men's minds which they can leave to future ages; and in particular it gave a new importance to architecture and all the applied arts, since, being produced by cooperation and for purposes of use, they express the general state of mind better than those arts, such as painting, which are altogether the work of individual artists. All this Ruskin saw; and he saw that the building and applied art of his own time were bad as they had never been before. And this badness troubled him as if it were something corrupt and sinister in the manners of men and women about him. It was not merely that he missed a pleasure which other ages enjoyed; he also was aware of a positive evil from which they had been free. Art for him was not a mere superfluity that men could have or not as they chose; it was a quality of all things made by men, which must be good or bad, and which expressed some goodness or badness in them. So, from being a critic of art, he became a critic of society, and, after writing about old buildings and modern painters, he wrote about political economy, about the order and disorder of that society which produced all the ugliness of his own time.

Now many men before him had denounced the evils of their day; but he was the first to be turned into a prophet by aesthetic discontent, and the fact that he was so turned

2. **William Morris** and **William Frend De Morgan** (for the design) and **Architectural Pottery Co.** (for the production),
Panel of tiles, 1876.
Slip-covered tiles, hand-painted in various colours, glazed on earthenware blanks, 160 x 91.5 cm.
Victoria & Albert Museum, London.

3. *Tulip and Trellis*, 1870.
   Hand-painted in blue and green on tin-glazed
   earthenware tile, 15.3 x 15.3 cm.
   Victoria & Albert Museum, London.

was one of great significance. He was a genius who detected a new danger to the life of man and who expressed an uneasiness spreading among the population, though he alone was conscious of it. He was and remained a critic, one who experienced and reasoned about his experiences rather than one who created. His rebellion was one of thought rather than of action, and the discoveries that he made had still to be confirmed by actual experiment. It was possible for men to say of him that he was a pure theorist; and indeed he often theorised rashly and wilfully and made many glaring errors of fact. He had the intuition of genius but not the knowledge of practice; he seemed often to speak with more eloquence than authority.

But he was followed in his rebellion by another man of genius who was by nature not a critic but an artist, that is to say, a man whose chief desire was to make things and to express his own values in the making of them. As Ruskin turned from the criticism of works of art to the criticism of society, so William Morris turned from the making of works of art to the effort to remake society. The biographer Mackail has said of him that he devoted the whole of his extraordinary powers towards no less an object than the reconstitution of the civilised life of mankind. That is true, and it had never been true of any artist before him; at least no artist had ever been turned from his art to politics because he was an artist. Morris was so turned; and for that reason he is the chief representative of that æsthetic discontent which is peculiar to that time.

One might have expected that he would be the last man to feel it; since he could himself make whatever beautiful things he wanted. Not only could he express his desire for beauty in poetry, but he could also express his own ideas of beauty in the work of his hands. However ugly the world outside him might be, he could make an earthly Paradise for himself, and could enjoy all the happiness of the artist in doing so. There are some men of great gifts who can never be content with their exercise; but Morris was as happy in making any of the hundred different things that he made so well as a child is happy at play. He knew early in life what he wanted to do; and he was as free as any man could be to do it.

4. **William Morris** (for the design?) and **Architectural Pottery Co.** (for the production), *Four Pink and Hawthorn Tiles*, 1887. Slip-covered, hand-painted in colours and glazed on earthenware blanks, 15.5 x 15 cm. Victoria & Albert Museum, London.

Introduction

At the age of twenty-one he became his own master, with a comfortable fortune. His father was dead; and, though his mother had cherished the hope that he would become a bishop, she suffered her disappointment quietly. He began at once to practice several arts, and satisfied both himself and the public in his practice of them. So he had no quarrel with the world so far as his own well-being was concerned; indeed he can be compared, for universal good fortune, only with his famous contemporary Leo Tolstoy. And he was like Tolstoy too in this, that his private happiness could neither enervate nor satisfy him. Some men rebel against society because they are unhappy; but Tolstoy and Morris put away their happiness to rebel. Each of them in his own earthly Paradise, heard the voice of unhappiness outside it; each saw evil in the world which made his own good intolerable to him.

They rebelled for different reasons; and to many they have both seemed irrational in their rebellion, for they were both drawn from work for which they had genius to work for which they had none. Tolstoy was not born to be a saint, nor was Morris born to be a revolutionary, and the world has lamented the perverse waste of natural powers which their rebellion caused. Indeed, in the case of Morris it has seemed to many that he quarreled with the world on a trivial point. To them art is a pleasant ornament of life; but if, for some reason, it is one that society at present cannot excel in, they are well content to do without it, much more content than they would be to do without golf or sport. To them Morris is merely a man who made a great fuss about his own particular line of business. Naturally there was nothing like leather to him; but men in another line of business cannot be expected to pay much heed to him.

Morris himself, however, held that art is everybody's business, whether they are themselves artists or not. And by art he, like Ruskin, did not mean merely pictures or statues. Indeed, he thought little of these compared with all the work of men's hands that used to be beautiful in the past and now is ugly. The ugliness of houses, tables and chairs, clothes, cups and saucers, in fact of everything that men made, whether they tried to make it beautiful or were content that it should be ugly – this universal ugliness at first troubled him like a physical discomfort without his knowing why. And at first he, being himself a man of action and an artist, merely tried to make beautiful things for himself and others. But gradually he came to see that this single artistic effort of his would avail nothing in a world of ugliness, that all the conditions of our society favoured ugliness and thwarted beauty. He saw, too, from his own experience, that beauty was a symptom of happy work and ugliness of unhappy; and so he became aware that, our society was troubled by a new kind of discontent, which it expressed in the ugliness of all that it made.

This he knew, as no one else knew it, from his own happiness in his work and the beauty through which he expressed it. If he had been a poet alone, he might never have known it except as a theory of Ruskin's; but being a worker in twenty different crafts he knew it more surely than Ruskin himself; and the knowledge became intolerable to him, so that he seemed to himself to be a mere idler while he was only

5. **William Frend De Morgan** (for the design) and **Sands End Pottery** (for the production), Panel, 1888-1897.
Buff-coloured earthenware, with painting over a white slip, 61.4 x 40.5 cm.
Victoria & Albert Museum, London.

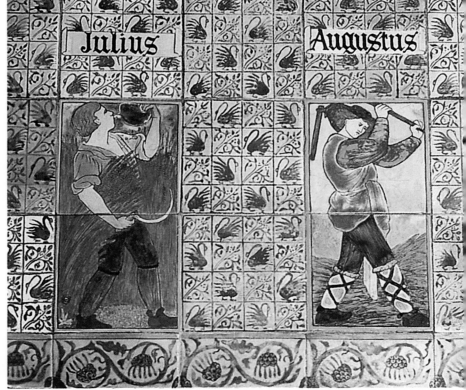

6. *The Months of the Year*, 1863-1864.

Hand-painted tiles.

Old Hall, Queens College, Cambridge.

Of a certain Prince who delivered a King's daughter from a sleep of a hundred years, wherein she & all hers had been cast by enchantment

doing his own work and enjoying his own happiness in it. He could not rest until he had tried to show other men the happiness they had lost, whether they were rich or poor, whether they were toiling without joy themselves or living on the joyless labour of others. Many men have rebelled against society and have preached rebellion because of the fearful contrast between riches and poverty; but it was not poverty that made Morris rebel so much as the nature of the work, which in our time most poor men have to do. He believed that their work was joyless as it never had been before; and that, not poverty, was to him the peculiar evil of their time against which, as a workman himself, he rebelled and wished the poor to rebel. They knew, of course, that they were poor, but they were not aware of this peculiar penalty of their poverty; and he was determined to make both them and the rich aware of it. He would open men's eyes to the meaning of his prevailing ugliness. He would make the rich see that they too were poorer than a peasant of the thirteenth century, in that there was no beauty of their own time in which they could take delight as if it were a general happiness, but only an ugliness that must dispirit them like a general unhappiness.

So he turned from his art to preach to men like a prophet; the value of his preaching lay in the fact that he was attacking a new evil that had grown up while men were unaware of it. And because the evil was new, they paid little attention to him at first; for men are as conservative in their discontents as in other things, and civilisation is always being threatened by new dangers while they are thinking of the old. To Morris the chief danger of our civilisation seemed to be the growth of a barbarism caused by joyless labour and of a discontent that did not know its cause. He feared lest the great mass of men should gradually come to believe that our society was not worth the sacrifices that were made for it; indeed, he sometimes hoped that it would be destroyed by this belief. Yet he was determined to do his best to save it, if it could be saved and transformed. For, as Mackail puts it, he believed that it could not be saved except by a reconstitution of the civilised life of mankind. The rich must learn to love art more than riches, and the poor to hate joyless work more than poverty. There must be a change in values that would mean a change of heart; and Morris did not despair of that change. Yet he knew that he was alone in his efforts to bring it about; for though he consorted and worked with other Socialists, his desires and hopes, and therefore his methods, were different from theirs. They were, many of them, able and devoted men who hoped by means of organisation to change the economic structure of society so that there should be no more very rich or very poor. Among these he was like a saint among ecclesiastics; for he desired something far beyond a more equal distribution of wealth, and he would not have been at all content with a world in which men lived and worked as they do now but without extreme poverty or riches. Other Socialists protested against the present waste of our superfluous energy; he told men what they might do with their superfluous energy when they had ceased to waste it. There is a common notion, favoured by the books of writers like Bellamy, that a Socialist state would be dull, with every one living as people live now in a prosperous middle-class suburb. Indeed, Bellamy tells us with prophetic rapture that in his Utopia there will be no need of umbrellas since there will be porticos over all the side-ways in every town.

7. **Edward Burne-Jones** and **Lucy Faulkner**,
   Sleeping Beauty, 1862-1865.
   Hand-painted on tin-glazed earthenware tiles,
   76.2 x 120.6 cm.
   Victoria & Albert Museum, London.

8. *Ariadne*, 1870.
   Polished ceramic tile.
   Victoria & Albert Museum, London.

9. *Angels*, undated.
   Tile Panel.
   St John the Baptist Church, Findon, Sussex.

10. **Edward Burne-Jones** and **Lucy Faulkner**,
    Cinderella, 1863.
    Tile panel, overglazed polychrome decoration
    on tin-glazed Dutch earthenware blanks in
    ebonized oak frame, 71 x 153 cm.
    Walker Art Gallery, Liverpool.

But Morris wanted something more in a reorganised society than a municipal substitute for umbrellas. It is one of the worst failures of our society that it has forgotten pleasure for comfort; that it thinks more of the armchair than of the dance. Morris tried to make men wish, like himself, for pleasure more than for comfort, and in the Utopia that he dreamt of, there were armchairs for the old, no doubt, but dancing for the young. Indeed, in his ideal state all life and all labour would be a kind of dance rather than a comfortable and torpid repose. That is to say, every activity of man would be made delightful by the superfluous energy of a civilised fellowship. We should enjoy our common work, as the craftsmen of the thirteenth century must have enjoyed building a great cathedral together; and our enjoyment would manifest itself in the beauty of all that we made. That was what Socialism meant to him, and all its machinery was only a means to that end.

It is easy to call him a visionary; but visionaries are necessary to every great movement, because they alone can give it direction, and they alone can make men desire the goal towards which they move. It is not enough to preach peace by talking of the horrors of war; for men are so made that they prefer horrors to dullness. You must persuade them that peace means a fuller and more glorious life than war, if you would make them desire it passionately. Morris said that our present society was in a state of economic war, and that for that reason it was anxious, joyless and impotent, like the life of a savage tribe engaged in incessant vendettas. The economic peace which he desired was one in which men would have leisure and power to do all that was best worth doing; and he hoped to bring that peace about by filling them with his own desire to do what was best worth doing. And as the saint affects men more by his vision of Heaven than the ecclesiastics affect them with all their organisation and discipline, so, it may be, Morris has done more for Socialism than all the scientific Socialists. For he knew quite clearly what he wanted in life and no one can say that he wanted what was not desirable. The world distrusts philanthropists and reformers of all kinds because they do not in their own lives convince the world that they are good judges of happiness. If they want us to be like themselves, we look at them and decide that we do not want to be like them. But no one could know Morris or his way of life without wanting to be like him. No one could say that he set out to reform the world without having first made a good business of life himself. When he tells us how to be happy and why we miss happiness he speaks with authority and not as the philanthropists; indeed, his ideas of what life should be commend themselves to us even without his authority, and there are many now who share them without knowing their origin.

There was a time when the world was more interested in Morris's ideas than in Morris himself, and his influence was greater than his name. In his art he affected the art of all Europe so profoundly that what he did alone seems to be only the product of his age. As a poet he is commonly thought of as the last and most extreme of the romantics; but his later poetry, at least, is quite free from the romantic despair of reality and nearly all of it is free from romantic vagueness.

How her sisters would go to the Prince's feast without her, but her god-mother g[...]

OF THE FORTUNE OF THE MAID WHO WAS CAL[...]

How she lost her shoe of glass at the feast and how the Prince made to be cried that [...]

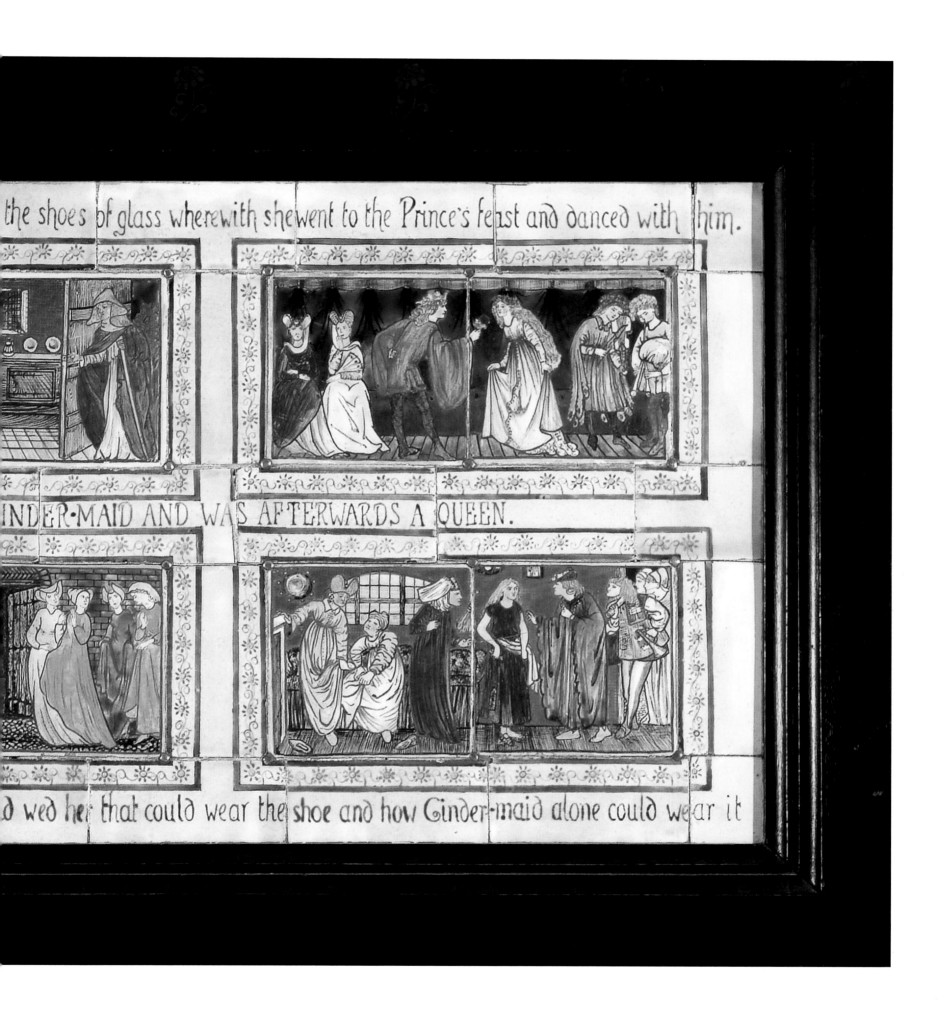

the shoes of glass wherewith she went to the Prince's feast and danced with him.

INDER-MAID AND WAS AFTERWARDS A QUEEN.

d wed her that could wear the shoe and how Cinder-maid alone could wear it

When Morris described the world that is not, he was, as it were, making plans of the world as he wished it to be; and he was always concerned with the future even when he seemed most absorbed in the past. In that respect he differed from all the other romantic poets, and in his most visionary poetry he tells us constantly what he valued in reality, what is best worth doing and being in life. All that he wrote, in verse or prose romance, is a tale of his own great adventure through a world that he wished to change; and we cannot yet tell how great a change he has worked or will work upon it. But we know already that he was one of the greatest men of the nineteenth century and, with Tolstoy, the most lonely and distinct of them all. In this book I have tried to give some description of his greatness rather than to write his life. He is the subject of a volume, not because he was a poet or an artist, but because the minds of men would have been different from what they are if he had never been born. Yet his art and his poetry were a great part of his action; indeed he was artist and poet before he had any conscious intention of changing the world, and the world has listened to his advice because he was an artist and a poet.

He was also, I believe, a greater and far more various poet than most people think. He is commonly known as a spinner of agreeable but shadowy romances, both in verse and in prose. I have therefore written at some length in the effort to show that he was far more than that. There are small men who have a specific gift for literature or art and whose work pleases us because of this gift, in spite of their smallness. But Morris was a great man, great in intelligence, in will, and in passion; and the better one knows his work, the more one sees that greatness in all of it. All those who knew him well recognised it, even if they cared nothing for poetry or art; they fell under his influence as men fell under the influence of Napoleon, and that although they had none of Napoleon's love of power. This book is written by someone who did not know him, and it is an attempt to show the nature of his influence and of his greatness in his works. He did so many things that it is impossible to speak of them all in a volume of this length; and he was never the centre of a circle like Doctor Johnson or Rossetti. Those who dealt directly with him felt that he made the issues of life and of art clearer to them; and that, we may be sure, he will continue to do for many generations yet unborn.

11. *Venus*, 1870.

   Miniature. Ink, gouache and guilding on paper,
   27.9 x 21.6 cm.
   Victoria & Albert Museum, London.

12. **Anonymous**, *Nobleman* (probably Wolfert
   Van Borssel) from the *Metamorphoses*,
   late 15th century.
   Parchment, 45 x 33.5 cm.
   Private collection, Bruges.

13. **Dante Gabriel Rossetti**,

   Beatrice Meeting Dante at a Marriage Feast,
   Denies Him Her Salutation, 1855.
   Watercolour on paper, 34 x 42 cm.
   Ashmolean Museum, Oxford.

The Early Years, A Promising Future

Childhood and Youth

William Morris was born at Walthamstow on March 24, 1834. There was nothing in the circumstances of his childhood to make him unlike other men of his class. His father was partner in a prosperous firm of bill-brokers and the family remained well-to-do after his death in 1847. Morris's childhood was happy but not remarkable. He gave no special proofs of genius, but showed the same character and tastes as in later years. He liked to wander about Epping Forest and knew the names of birds, learnt whatever he wished to learn easily and remembered it exactly, and was both passionate and good-natured.

One story told of him shows what he wished to learn and how well he remembered it. At the age of eight he saw the Church of Minster in Thanet, and fifty years afterwards, not having seen it since, he was able to describe it in detail. This is one proof, among many, that he understood Gothic art as the child Mozart understood music, seeming to recognise in it a language that he knew by nature. This process of recognition continued all through his youth. It was the chief part of his education; it was what distinguished him from other youths of his time; and it was, as we can see now, a sign of his strong natural character and a preparation for the whole of his future life.

To Morris a Gothic building was not merely something beautiful or romantic or strange. He did not enjoy it only as most of us enjoy a beautiful tune. It had for him that more precise meaning which music had for the young Mozart. He saw not only that it was the kind of art he liked, but also why he liked it. For it expressed to him, more clearly than words, a state of being which he felt to be desirable. It was as if the men who had made it were before him in the flesh and he saw them and loved them. Indeed he had that passionate liking for the whole society in which the great works of Gothic art were produced which some of us have for our favourite poets or musicians. And he missed Gothic art from his present as if it were the voice of some dead loved one. Church after church, as he first saw them in his youth, was remembered as if it were the first meeting with a dear friend; and it was fixed in his mind, not only because he enjoyed its beauty, but because it expressed for him that state of being which he loved in it. It was like a face vividly remembered through affection, and all its details were connected with each other in his mind as if they were features.

We must understand this if we are to understand Morris's early passion for the Middle Ages and all their works. It was not the dry passion of the mere archaeologist who

14. *Rose*, 1883.
    Printed cotton.
    Private collection.

15. *Violet and Columbine*, 1883.
    Pattern for woven textile.
    Private collection.

16. *Rose* (detail), 1883.
    Pencil, pen, ink and watercolour on paper,
    90.6 x 66.3 cm.
    Victoria & Albert Museum, London.

17. *Cray*, 1884.
    Printed cotton, 96.5 x 107.9 cm.
    Victoria & Albert Museum, London.

studies the past because it is dead. Morris studied it because he saw it alive. The churches for him were not old, but just built. It was the later buildings of what he called the age of ignorance that to him seemed obsolete, for they expressed nothing that he wanted. Just as the minds of the great artists of the Renaissance leapt back over an intervening time to classical art, so his mind leapt back to the Gothic and found in it the new world that he wished to create.

At the age of thirteen he was sent to Marlborough College, then a new school and lax in its discipline. This was a piece of good fortune for him, for he did not need to be set either to work or to play. He was not an aimless idler, to be kept out of mischief by compulsory games. At Marlborough he had another forest, to roam through and a library of books to read. He had not been taught any craft in childhood; but his fingers were as busy as his mind; and for want of some better employment he exercised them in endless netting, as he exercised his mind by telling endless tales of adventure to his schoolmates. At Marlborough he became aware of the High Church Movement and was drawn into it, so that when he left the school knowing, as he said, most of what was to be known about English Gothic, he went to Exeter College, Oxford with the intention of taking Orders.

This was in the Lent term of 1853; and while at Oxford he continued to educate himself much as he had done at school. At Exeter, we are told, there was then neither teaching nor discipline Morris's tutor described him as a rather rough unpolished youth who exhibited no special literary tastes nor capacity, from which we may guess that they were not close friends. Indeed Morris all his life used the word don as a term of abuse more severe than many strong-sounding words at his

command. But Oxford itself, still unblemished in its beauty, delighted him; and he got from it his first notion of what a city should be. Yet it seemed to him a misused treasure of the past, for already he desired a present capable of expressing itself with the same energy and beauty. The present of Oxford seemed to him a mere barbarism, frivolous and pedantic; but for one friend whom he made in his first term, he might have lived a lonely life there. This friend was Edward Burne-Jones, a freshman from King Edward's Grammar School, Birmingham, who already promised much as an artist, but who, like Morris, meant to take Orders. Neither of them cared much for the undergraduates of Exeter; but there were some of Burne-Jones's schoolfellows at Pembroke to whom he introduced Morris, and among whom Morris got the society he needed. Canon Dixon, the poet, who was one of these, tells us that at first they regarded Morris simply as a pleasant boy who was fond of talking, which he did in a husky shout:

"He was very fond of sailing a boat. He was also exceedingly fond of single-stick and a good fencer... But his mental qualities, his intellect also, began to be perceived and acknowledged. I remember Faulkner remarking to me, 'How Morris seems to know things, doesn't he?' And then it struck me that it was so. I observed how decisive he was: how accurate, without any effort or formality. What an extraordinary power of observation lay at the base of his casual or incidental remarks, and how many things he knew that were quite out of our way, as, for example architecture."

In this new world of people and things and ideas Morris was not bewildered or misled by momentary influences. Then, as afterwards, he seemed to know by instinct what he wanted to learn and where he could find it. He had a scent for his own future, little as he knew yet what it was to be; and whatever he did or read was a preparation for it. Already there had begun in England that reaction against all the ideas of our industrial civilisation which Morris himself was to carry further than any. But the ideas were still predominant and were commonly supposed to have a scientific consistency and truth against which only wilfulness could rebel. Yet there was this curious inconsistency in them – that, while they recommended a certain course of action to society which it was to adopt of its own free will, they promised as the mechanical result of that action a state of moral and material well-being to which society would attain without further effort. The will was to make its choice at the start; and then no further choice would be required of it. But this inconsistency was also based upon certain assumptions that do not now seem to us beyond dispute. It was assumed, for instance, that the main end of every society was to become rich; and that it would become rich if individuals were allowed to acquire riches by any means they chose to employ. This license was called freedom; and indeed it meant a complete freedom for those who were rich already, but a freedom merely nominal and legal for those who were poor. They were free to be rich if they could; but the great mass of them could not, and remained in extreme poverty, in spite or rather because of the riches of the few. Thus the national well-being promised did not come about, although great fortunes were made; and the moral well being also failed to equal expectations. Indeed there was an inconsistency between the morality of the individual and the morality of society that was bad for both. The morality of

18. *Wandle*, 1884.
   Indigo-discharged and block-printed cotton,
   160.1 x 96.5 cm.
   Victoria & Albert Museum, London.

19. *Rose*, 1877.
   Colours prints from woodblocks.
   Victoria & Albert Museum, London.

20. *Wandle*, 1884.
   Indigo-discharged and block-printed cotton,
   165 x 92 cm.
   Victoria & Albert Museum, London.

the individual was still supposed to be Christian, except when he was making money. But, as soon as he began to do that he was regarded as a member of a society whose aim only was to make money. Then his Christian morality was superseded by an economic law against which it was merely sentimental to rebel. This kind of inconsistency has always existed; but it has never been so glaring or produced so much moral and intellectual

confusion as in England in the nineteenth century. Then it was that we established our reputation as a nation of hypocrites and were confirmed in our national dislike of logic. The great mass of Englishmen wished to be good, according to the Christian pattern; but they also wished to make money and they acquired a notion, implied in their laws and in their habits of thought if never openly stated, that money was the material reward of goodness. But this notion was always proving itself to be untrue. The rich were not identical with the good according to any system of morality known to man, least of all according to the Christian. Yet they were favoured and encouraged by all the laws, and by all the anarchy, of the State. If any one pointed out this inconsistency, he was told that the State, having made its wise choice in favour of riches, had no further choice in the matter. Scientific laws were now operating in favour of the rich and against the poor, and they were no more to be resisted than the law of gravity.

Meanwhile certain people asked themselves how they liked this society, which was settling into a second state of nature; they found that they did not like it at all. Carlyle, for instance, disliked it as much as Jonah disliked Nineveh. In particular he disliked the rich because they were sheltered against reality by the whole structure of society, and because in their shelter they talked and thought about unreal things. He was as sure as Jonah that God in his wrath would some day blow all their comfort away from them; but he had no notion of a civilisation to take the place of that which he wished to destroy, nor of a peace of mind to succeed the complacent torpor against which he raged. His aim was to reduce the minds of men to the first stage of conversion, to that utter humiliation in which they might hear the sudden voice of God. We are used to his denunciations; but to Morris they were new and they assured him that he was right in his own instinctive dislike of all that Carlyle denounced.

As previously mentioned, Ruskin's rebellion was at first æsthetic; it was a rebellion not merely against the art of his own time, but against all the art of the Renaissance and the ideas expressed in that art. The *Stones of Venice* was published in Morris's first year at Oxford; and from the chapter on the Nature of Gothic he learnt that there was reason in

his own love of Gothic and dislike of Renaissance architecture. Ruskin points out that in Gothic every workman had a chance of expressing himself, whereas in Renaissance, and in all architecture since, the workman only did exactly what the architect told him to do. Thus Gothic missed the arrogant and determined perfection of Renaissance, but it had an eager life and growth of its own, like that of a State, which recognises the human rights of all its members. There were, of course, different tasks for all the workmen according to their ability, but each to some extent expressed his own will in what he did. To Morris this chapter was a gospel and all his own ideas about art grew out of it; indeed he was unjust to the art of the Renaissance, not merely through a caprice of personal taste, but because it seemed to him that at the Renaissance European society had taken a wrong turn, arriving at the dull follies of the industrial age. He knew, of course, that there were great artists during the Renaissance, but in their work he saw a foreboding of what was to come of it. For him it expressed, however splendidly, a state of mind that seemed wrong, and he refused to be dazzled by the triumphs of Michelangelo, as by the victories of Napoleon.

If he had been a critic, this prejudice of his against the Renaissance would have been a mere prejudice harmful to his work; but he was to be an artist, and afterwards a revolutionary, that is to say a man of action on both stages. Therefore he rightly and naturally judged all art and all ideas by their practical value to himself. And even when he was an undergraduate at Oxford he saw what would be of practical value to him. He knew already what he wanted both in life and in art and he had only to learn how to do and to get what he wanted.

In the long vacation of 1854 he went abroad, for the first time, to Northern France and Belgium, where he saw the greatest works of Gothic architecture and the paintings of Van Eyck and Memling. He said long afterwards that the first sight of Rouen was the greatest pleasure he had ever known; and Van Eyck and Memling remained always his favorite painters, no doubt because their art was still the art of the Middle Ages practiced with a new craft and subtlety.

In the same year he came of age and inherited an income of £900 a year. Thus he was already his own master and his freedom only determined him to make the best possible use of it. In the next year he and Burne-Jones finally resolved to be artists not clergymen. Morris had been drawn into the High Church Movement, no doubt because it was part of the general reaction against modern materialism and ugliness. But the beliefs which were forming in his mind were not religious, however harmonious with the true Christian faith. He changed his purpose not in any violent reaction against it, but because he had a stronger desire to do something else. He had already begun to write poetry, which he did quite suddenly and with immediate success. Canon Dixon tells how he went one evening to Exeter and found Morris with Burne-Jones. As soon as he entered the room. Burne-Jones exclaimed wildly, "'He's a great poet.' 'Who is?' asked we. 'Why, Topsy.'" Then Morris read them *The Willow and the Red Cliff*, the first poem he had ever written in his life. Dixon expressed his admiration and Morris replied, "Well, if this is poetry, it is very easy to write." "From that time onward," says Dixon, "for a term or two, he came to my rooms almost every day with a new poem."

21. *Little Flowers.*
Pattern for chintz.
Victoria & Albert Museum, London.

22. **Edward Burne-Jones**, **William Morris** and
John Henry Dearle (for the design) and
Morris & Co. (for the production), *Holy Grail*
Tapestry – Quest for the Holy Grail Tapestries –
The Arming and Departure of the Knights (II),
1895-1896.
High warp tapestry, wool and silk weft on
cotton warp, 360 x 244 cm.
Birmingham Museums & Art Gallery,
Birmingham.

Morris destroyed many of his early poems, but some pieces and fragments remain of them and they are, as Dixon thought when he first heard them, quite unlike any other poetry. We can believe, too, that they were easy to write, for they sound as if they had come into his mind as tunes come into the minds of musicians:

> Christ keep the Hollow Land
> All the summer-tide;
> Still we cannot understand
> Where the waters glide;
> Only dimly seeing them
> Coldly slipping through
> Many green-lipped cavern-mouths,
> Where the hills are blue.

Morris afterwards became the best storyteller of all our modern poets; but because he had this power of making verse that was almost musical, verse that needed no context or preparation but cast an instant spell upon the mind through the ear, he was always a poet as well as a storyteller. In his life as in his poetry there was the same contrast and yet harmony of the visionary and the practical, and the same power of making the one serve the other. At this time in his poetry he was a pure visionary. Things that delighted his eyes or his mind came into his verse as such things come into dreams. He might, no doubt, have cultivated this poetry of the sub-consciousness; but he was not long content to be only a visionary either in life or in art. It may be that the prose romances, which he began to write in 1855, gave him a disgust of this kind of writing. They too are unlike anything else in English literature, but far inferior to the poems. For that vagueness of sense, which in the verse is combined with a curious intensity of sound, bewilders and disappoints in a prose story, the more so because the style is uncertain and not always suited to the subject. Indeed at this time Morris wrote prose as minor poets write verse, seeming now and then to adopt a sentimental character not his own and to express what he wanted to feel rather than what he did feel. Thirty years later, when he again began writing prose, he was a complete master of it; but in 1855 he first read Chaucer and was turned back from prose to verse, and to verse about subjects he chose consciously.

He and his friends had a young and generous desire to work some great change upon the world. They had vague notions of founding a brotherhood, they saw that the condition of the poor was horrible, they wanted to do something at once; and, not knowing precisely what they wanted to do, they naturally determined to start a magazine. Dixon first proposed it to Morris in 1855 and the whole set were delighted with the idea. Since they had friends at Cambridge they determined that these too should write for it; and so, when it came into being, it was called the *Oxford and Cambridge Magazine,* though it was nearly all written by Oxford men. The first issue appeared on January 1, 1856, and it ran for twelve issues, appearing monthly. Morris financed and wrote eighteen poems, romances and articles for it. No other contributor came near him in merit except Dante Gabriel Rossetti, whom Burne-Jones had met at the end of 1855 and who already admired Morris's poetry. Both Tennyson and Ruskin praised the magazine; but it sold few issues, confirming the fears of Ruskin, who said that he had never known an honest journal get on yet.

23. **Dante Gabriel Rossetti**,

Before the Battle, 1858, retouched in 1862.
Transparent and opaque watercolour on paper,
mounted on canvas, 41.4 x 27.5 cm.
The Museum of Fine Arts, Boston.

24. *La Belle Iseult*, 1858.
Oil on canvas, 71.8 x 50.2 cm.
Tate Gallery, London.

The Influence of Rossetti

In 1855 Morris took his degree, and in January 1856 he was articled to George Edmund Street, one of the chief architects of the Gothic Revival and the designer of the Law Courts. He was, as Morris said, "a good architect as things go now"; but he produced imitation Gothic under conditions utterly different from those in which the real Gothic had grown, and it was impossible that Morris should be satisfied with the work he did or should wish to do work like it. Morris became his pupil, no doubt, because he was more interested in architecture than in any other art; but he was not born to be an architect, at least under conditions at that time. This he soon discovered, but in Street's office he learnt some useful things and met Philip Webb, who was afterwards the chief figure, not in the Gothic Revival, but in the revival of architecture. Webb became one of his closest friends and they co-operated in many works of art.

Nowadays we have art students instead of apprentices; and there is always a danger that the student, even if he is articled to an architect, will spend too long in learning instead of doing. Morris from the first was not content to be a mere student. Besides working hard in his office he began to model in clay, to carve in wood and stone, and to illuminate, on his own account. And though he was his own teacher in these arts and in many others, he seemed to know by instinct the right way of practicing them and wasted no time in mistaken experiments. This instinctive tightness, which was a kind of natural sagacity applied to the arts, was the secret of his versatility. He might vary in the quality of his work, but it was never wrong in intention; and therefore he never had to unlearn what he had learnt.

Until then Morris had never met a great man and had gone his own way unaffected by any strong personal influence; but in London he met Rossetti, who was teaching Burne-Jones to paint, and of the many men who fell under Rossetti's spell he, perhaps, was the most completely subdued by it. We can admire Rossetti's poetry and pictures; but to those who knew him he seemed far greater than anything that he did. Or rather they saw in his works all that magic of the man himself which is dead to us. He could tell what he wanted to do in such a way that it seemed to be done and also seemed to be the only thing worth doing in the world. When Morris and Burne-Jones first knew him he was at the height of his powers. His ambition was to do for the art of painting what the Romantic poets had done for poetry, i.e., to quicken it with passion and with the beauty that comes of passion clearly expressed. While in France the impressionist painters were trying to represent a new order of facts, Rossetti in England was trying to express in painting a new state of mind. He was not content with poetic subjects, like the dull illustrators of the time; he wished also to treat them poetically like the great Italian primitives. To Burne-Jones and Morris he seemed to be transforming the art of painting, giving to it that purpose and intensity, which they hoped, were soon to quicken the whole of society. They lived in the expectation that great things were about to happen in the world; and here already they were happening in art. What

25. *The Adoration of the Magi*, 1888.
Tapestry woven in wool, silk and mohair on a cotton warp, 345.3 x 502.9 cm.
Castle Museum, Norwich.

Ruskin taught, Rossetti did and made others do; and, as Morris and Burne-Jones cared more for art than for anything else, he seemed to them a Messiah who could show them, and the world if it would listen, the way to salvation. Eager youth both desires and believes that the problems of life may be made quite simple for it; and it will therefore submit itself utterly to a hero who seems to simplify them. Rossetti, who cared for nothing but art, offered the promise of simplification; and for some years Morris was, as it were, in love with him. When Burne-Jones said that he feared to become a mere imitator of Rossetti, Morris replied: "I have got beyond that. I want to imitate Gabriel as much as I can."

Rossetti wished every one to be a painter. "If a man has any poetry in him," he said, "he should paint, for it has all been said and written and they have scarcely begun to paint it." Therefore, though he admired Morris's poetry, he told him that he too must be a painter. Morris wrote in a letter:

> "Rossetti says I ought to paint. [...] He says I shall be able; now as he is a very great man and speaks with authority and not as the Scribes, I must try... so I am going to try, not giving up architecture, but trying if it is possible to get six hours a day for drawing besides office work. [...] I can't enter into politico-social subjects with any interest, for on the whole I see that things are in a muddle, and I have no power or vocation to set them right in ever so little a degree. My work is the embodiment of dreams in one form or another."

Here he says in prose just what he was still saying twelve years later in verse: "Dreamer of dreams, born out of my due time, why should I strive to set the crooked straight?"

But even in this determination to forget the evils of the world and in this very insistence that he is a dreamer, we can see the beginnings of the conflict that was to shake his life. Rossetti did not call himself a dreamer; for to him art was the chief reality. Morris now was trying to make it the chief reality for himself, but he could not separate it from other things; and in the end it was art, and his hopes and fears for it, that drew him out of his shadowy isle of bliss.

At present, however, Rossetti's word was law; and since Rossetti told him to be a painter he became one. He finished little, but his *Queen Guenevere*, also called *La Belle Iseult*, is one of the finest of all Pre Raphaelite pictures and equal in merit to his poem, the *Defence of Guenevere*. Yet he said that the frame of a picture always bothered him, and this saying expresses the whole difference between him and Rossetti. For Rossetti art was always in a frame and made more intense by its very isolation. It was something into which you escaped from life; but Morris rather wanted to turn all life into art and enjoyed the triumph of art most when it glorified things of use. For him, though he soon gave up the purpose of being an architect, the great art was always architecture; for in that he saw use made beautiful and the needs of men

26. **Edward Burne-Jones** and **William Morris** (for the design) and **Morris & Co.** (for the production), *Pomona*, 1885.
Tapestry woven wool, silk and mohair on a cotton warp, 300 x 210 cm.
The Whitworth Gallery,
University of Manchester, Manchester.

27. **William Morris** and **John Henry Dearle** (for the design) and **Morris, Marshall, Faulkner & Co.** (for the production), *The Orchard* or *The Seasons*, c. 1863.
Tapestry woven wool, silk and mohair on a cotton warp, 221 x 472 cm.
Victoria & Albert Museum, London.

I am the ancient apple-queen · as once I was so am I now ·
for evermore a hope unseen · betwixt the blossom and the bough ·

ah where's the river's hidden gold · and where the windy grave of troy ·
yet come I as I came of old · from out the heart of summer's joy ·

45

Orchard, or The Seasons. Tapestry. 1890. Manufactured by Morris & Co. Designed by William Morris, with figures by John Henry Dearle. Victoria and Albert Museum, London.

ennobled by their manner of satisfying them. And all the art that he most loved, at first by instinct and afterwards on principle, was of the same nature as architecture and distinguished by the same kind of excellence. What we call decorative art was more than decoration to him. It pleased him like a smile of happiness, for he felt in it the well being both of the artist and of those for whom he worked. To Rossetti art was the expression of the artist's more peculiar emotions; and this he found most intense and complete in isolated works of art such as pictures. But Morris always saw in a work of art the relation between the artist and his public; and it was for him a social business that could not be well practiced except in a healthy society. This view of art was not a mere theory for him; it came to him through his own experience and he made a theory of it because his reason confirmed his instinct. He began by loving all Gothic art because of its noble submission to architecture; and he could not feel the same love for the art of the Renaissance when it became independent of architecture. There was egotism in it that displeased him and which seemed to him, when he came to think about it, a symptom of all the egotistical heresies of the modern world. With all his passion for art he was not inclined to glorify the artist or to conceive of him as a superman producing masterpieces in his lonely pride. He thought of him rather as a workman who gave more than was asked of him from love of his work. He knew well enough, of course, that Michelangelo and Velasquez were great men; but he judged the art of an age rather by its cottages and its cups and saucers than by its great pictures, as he judged the prosperity of a state by the condition of its poor rather than of its rich.

Thus it was certain that Rossetti would not remain master of his mind; but for the moment Morris obeyed him with the joy of one for whom all the problems of life are made easy by absolute obedience. He took rooms with Burne-Jones at 17, Red Lion Square, where Rossetti had lived before; and there they lived together a life about which many stories are told, working and playing with equal vigor and always under the spell of Rossetti. Yet already Morris began to do something on his own account which showed the natural bent of his mind. Their rooms were to be furnished and

Morris could not find in any shop a single new table or chair that he could endure. This was not mere fastidiousness. To him vulgarity in furniture was, like vulgarity of manners, the expression of a wrong state of mind; and if his own furniture had been vulgar, he would have felt responsible for it as for his own manners. Therefore he designed furniture to please himself, making drawings that were carried out by a carpenter. Thus simply and naturally he began his business of "poetic upholsterer." Not being able to get what he wanted from the minds of others, he got it from his own. This was his way all his life and the reason why he practiced so many arts in turn. He found them all either dead or corrupted; and, instead of complaining that the times were out of joint, he did what he could to set them right. From the first he was not only an artist, but one who tried to make the world what he wished it to be; beginning with armchairs he ended with society.

In the summer of 1857 Rossetti conceived the project of painting the new Debating Hall of the Oxford Union and obtained leave to do so with the help of other artists of his own choosing. There were to be ten paintings in tempera, all of subjects from the *Morte d'Arthur*; and the ceiling above them was to be decorated. Returning to London he told Burne-Jones and Morris that they were to start on the work at once. Other artists chosen were Arthur Hughes, Spencer-Stanhope, Val Prinsep and John Hungerford Pollen, all young men who would do whatever Rossetti commanded. None of them knew anything about mural painting, and some were only painters because Rossetti had ordered them to paint. The new walls were damp and not prepared in any way to receive colour; but no one had any misgivings. Morris, of course, would much rather paint a wall than a canvas; and he was in Oxford and had begun his picture before the others had made their designs. His subject was "How Sir Palomydes loved la Belle Iseult with exceeding great love out of measure". He filled the foreground with flowers, and Rossetti, who chaffed him as much as he admired him, suggested that he should fill the foreground of another picture with scarlet runners. Perhaps Morris remembered Blake's poem, "*O Sunflower, weary of time*", with its "youth pined away with desire." At any rate this was the beginning of the sunflower's artistic career; and Morris himself, no doubt, was heartily sick of it as an æsthetic symbol twenty-five years later. He was the first to finish as he had been to begin; and at once set to work to paint the roof. In this his old Oxford friends Faulkner and Dixon helped him. For Rossetti believed that any one, when he liked, could paint, and indeed he could communicate talent to his disciples, as a great general can communicate courage to his soldiers. The roof was finished in November; but Rossetti's painting, *Lancelot's Vision of the Sangrail*, was never finished. To judge from the drawing it must have been the finest work he ever did; but it and all the other paintings soon moldered away, and less remains of them now than of Leonardo da Vinci's *Last Supper*. Morris redecorated the roof in 1875.

The failure of this spirited adventure must have made Morris feel the contrast between the science and organisation of the great ages of art and the ignorance and indiscipline of his own time. All Rossetti's genius and leadership were wasted upon the walls of the Union because he knew nothing of the craft of wall painting. Morris learnt himself, and taught

28. **John Henry Dearle** (for the design), **Edward Burne-Jones** (for the figures) and **Morris & Co.** (for the production), *Angeli Laudantes*, 1894.
Tapestry woven wool, silk and mohair on a cotton warp, 237.5 x 202 cm.
Victoria & Albert Museum, London.

29. **Dante Gabriel Rossetti**, *Dantis Amor*, 1860.
Oil on panel, 74.9 x 81.3 cm.
Tate Gallery, London.

30. **William Morris** and **Edward Burne-Jones**, *The Pilgrim Outside the Garden of Love*, c. 1893-1898.
Detail from embroidered frieze *The Romaunt of the Rose*, 155.9 x 306.7 cm.
Victoria & Albert Museum, London.

others, to regard every art as a craft with technical secrets that must be learnt before it could be well practiced. And already he was teaching himself the secrets of craft after craft.

"In all illumination and work of that kind, Rossetti said of him, he is quite unrivalled by anything modern that I know." Illuminating was never an archaistic fad for him, but an exercise of his talent more natural than picture painting. How natural, we can see from a verse which he wrote long afterwards lamenting how all the arts of the world were unknown to the poor of great towns.

> The singers have sung and the builders have built,
> The painters have fashioned their tales of delight;
> For what and for whom hath the world's book been gilded,
> When all is for these but the blackness of night?

But the painting at the Oxford Union must also have given him a taste of the delights of a great age of art, the heightened powers of companionship, the happy rivalry free from the rancor and cares of competition. There were wonderful evenings after their work, Rossetti still predominating; and among the undergraduates who visited them was the poet Algernon Swinburne of Balliol. Val Prinsep told of his first dinner with Rossetti, where he was introduced to Morris who spoke little. After dinner Rossetti said to Morris, "Top, read us one of your grinds." Morris refused at first, but Rossetti insisted; and, says Prinsep:

"The effect produced on my mind was so strong that to this day, forty years after, I can still recall the scene. Rossetti on the sofa, with large melancholy eyes fixed on Morris, the poet at the table reading and ever fidgeting with his watch-chain, and Burne-Jones working at a pen-and-ink drawing:

> 'Gold on her hair and gold on her feet,
> And gold where the hems of her kirtle meet,
> And a golden girdle round my sweet,
> Ah ! Qu'elle est belle La Marguerite,'

still seems to haunt me, and this other stanza:

> 'Swerve to the left, son Roger,' he said,
> When you catch his eyes through the helmet slit.
> Swerve to the left, then out at his head,
> And the Lord God give you joy of it.'

I confess I returned to the Mitre with my brain in a whirl."

These verses are from two poems, the *Eve of Crecy* and *The Judgment of God*, both of which were printed in the volume called the *Defence of Guenevere and other Poems*, which Morris published early in 1858.

31. **Morris, Marshall, Faulkner & Co.**,
Moon Room panel from
the Green Dining Room, 1863.
Victoria & Albert Museum, London.

32. **Morris, Marshall, Faulkner & Co.**,
Elderflowers Room panel from
the Green Dining Room, 1863.
Victoria & Albert Museum, London.

33. **Morris, Marshall, Faulkner & Co.**,
Gourds Room panel from
the Green Dining Room, 1863.
Victoria & Albert Museum, London.

The Founding of the Firm

Morris was now about to enter upon the happiest period of his life, a period in which every circumstance, as well as his own gifts and character, conspired to bring him felicity, and in which he achieved fame by doing what he most desired to do. There was no outward reason why this happiness should not have lasted all his life; but, like Tolstoy, he was too great to remain content with it, and, like him he was driven by his own mind beyond happiness to a harder and lonelier task.

Morris, while painting at Oxford, had made the acquaintance of a Miss Jane Burden, whom, because of her great beauty, he and Rossetti wished to paint. She sat for both of them, and Morris fell in love with her and became engaged to her soon after the *Defence of Guenevere* was published. They were married in Oxford in April 1859; and then Morris began to look for a house that would satisfy him. He wished for a house and everything in it according to his own taste. An old house and old furniture would not content him, because he desired an art of his own time and was eager to produce it himself. He therefore bought a piece of orchard and meadow on Bexley Heath in Kent, above the valley of the Cray; and there Philip Webb, who had just set up as an architect on his own account, built a house for him.

Though the arts do not flourish now, it is difficult to remember or imagine their desperate condition in 1860. At the time, nearly all building was subject to a single principle; and that was as wrong as it could be, for it was the principle of disguise. If a house was built of brick it was covered with stucco so that it might look like stone. Every one, of course, knew stucco from stone; but the mere effort at disguise was considered creditable and a sign of gentility. No one, of course, can have thought stucco, used thus, a beautiful material; but no one ever considered the question of its beauty or ugliness. It was chosen for its decency and for social, not æsthetic, reasons.

And there was the same principle of choice in all the applied arts. Towards the end of the Italian Renaissance these arts had been used by the great to express their power, pride and wealth. And since these were realities, the arts themselves had often a real splendour and vigour. One can see that a Renaissance Palace was built for a great prince who, at least, knew how to enjoy himself magnificently. In the palace, in its furniture and in its gardens, there is the expression of a certain state of being with which those who enjoyed it were content. They had lost the high passion for a celestial glory that expressed itself in the great churches of the Middle Ages and were determined to make for themselves private Heavens here and now; and they did succeed in making them so far as they could be made out of material things. This tradition of Renaissance splendour still dominated all the arts in 1860; but they expressed then splendour and a pride that no longer existed. There were, of course, rich people, but they did not know, like the Princes of the Renaissance, how to enjoy their riches; and the art that was provided for them was nothing but an advertisement of their wealth. They liked furniture upon which much time and labour had evidently

34. Bed Cover, 1876.
Linen embroided with silks, 190.5 x 166.4 cm.
Victoria & Albert Museum, London.

35. *Acanthus and Vine*, 1870.
Design for the tapestry *Cabbage and Vine*.
Pencil and watercolour, 181 x 136.2 cm.
Victoria & Albert Museum, London.

36. *Acanthus* (Original design), 1874.
Wallpaper design. Pencil, watercolour and bodycolour on paper, 81.5 x 65.2 cm.
Victoria & Albert Museum, London.

37. *Cabbage and Vine*, 1897.
First tapestry designed by Morris also
known as *Acanthus and Vine*.
Kelmscott Manor, Oxfordshire.

been spent, because it was costly; but they never asked themselves whether the time and labour had been spent in making the furniture ugly, for they did not wish to enjoy the furniture but only their awareness that they were able to pay for it. For those who were not rich art was employed to give the illusion that they were rich. Machinery had made it possible to produce cheap imitations of costly ornament, uglier even than the originals. No one can ever have enjoyed these with their natural senses; what they enjoyed, or tried to enjoy, was merely the illusion of riches produced by them. The sense of beauty, in itself quite a simple instinctive thing, had not entirely disappeared, as one might suppose; it had been degraded into a sense of propriety, so that people called those things beautiful which seemed to them proper to their social station. As for art, except in pictures, few were conscious of its existence. Most people thought of it as an obsolete activity which modern civilisation had outgrown. They could not see that, being thus purposeless and ignored, it still persisted, not consciously expressing anything that was worth expression, but merely betraying all the meanness and failures and impotent unrest of the industrial age. And even the most intelligent allowed this purposeless tell-tale art to be imposed upon them, just as good men, in evil times, submit to a morality of cowardice and cruel habits.

But Morris saw what this bad art meant just as if he were a being from another planet. It was not merely that he disliked it with his senses; he had a moral dislike for it as an expression of evil things, and to him its ugliness was of the same kind as the ugliness of manners servile and pretentious. He, after Ruskin, was the first to have a scientific understanding of his own likes and dislikes in art. Philosophers have talked about the arts for ages, but they have isolated them from other activities. Ruskin and Morris looked rather for their connection with other activities, and with the whole mind of the society that produces them. They saw that people whose values are wrong will betray the fact in their art, that a society which worships riches will express its idolatry even in its table legs and chandeliers. But Morris, being a man of action, was determined not to express an idolatry that he hated in his table-legs or in any detail of his house. He meant that house to express the kind of life that he wished to lead, a life orderly, busy, free from pretence, free too from aimless rebellions, and devoted to a high purpose.

When Lord Grimthorpe called him a poetic upholsterer he meant to express his contempt for a man who could take upholstery so seriously. Morris himself liked the phrase and thought it just. He thought upholstering and all the furniture of a house ought to be as expressive as poetry; and he began with his own home. If he had ended there, his enterprise would have had little importance, and at the time, no doubt, he did not see where it would lead him. But it was the beginning of a revolt still only in its initiation, and the end of which no man can foresee.

The house that Philip Webb built for Morris aimed at no beauties, exquisite or palatial, beyond the power of the builders of that time. It was unlike other houses of the period chiefly in its plainness and in the quality of its material. It was built of red brick and

38. *Lys Kidderminster.*
   Pattern for a Kidderminster carpet.
   Billiard Room, Wightwick Manor, West Midlands.

39. *Tulip and Rose*, 1876.
   Woven woollen triple cloth, 297 x 171 cm.
   Victoria & Albert Museum, London.

40. *Wey*, c. 1883.
   Furnishing fabric. Indigo-discharged, block-printed cotton, 85 x 110.5 x 4.5 cm (framed).
   Private collection.

roofed with red tiles, L shaped, and two stories high. It stood among apple and cherry trees, and was so placed that hardly a tree had to be cut down. Indeed, Mackail tells us, apples fell in at the windows as they stood open on hot August nights. The garden was planned as carefully as the house, being an outdoor continuation of it rather than a wilderness or a flower-show. A rose-trellis made a quadrangle with the two sides of the building; and in the midst of this was a well house of brick and oak with a round tiled roof like a low spire. Morris knew about gardening as about other domestic arts; and for him it was always a domestic art, not a horticultural game.

When the house was built Morris set to work to furnish it himself, and the difficulty of getting things made according to his own designs or the designs of his friends was the immediate cause of the foundation of the firm of Morris & Co. It is not certain who first proposed the enterprise, though it had long been in Morris's mind, but Rossetti, Madox Brown the painter, Burne-Jones and Webb were all parties to it. To them were added Faulkner, Morris's old College friend, and Peter Paul Marshall, a friend of Madox Brown, and a sanitary engineer. He never did much for the firm, but Faulkner worked hard for it, both as a man of business, and, to the best of his ability, as a craftsman.

The circular of the firm, which is headed Morris, Marshall, Faulkner & Co., insists upon the need of co-operation in all decorative art and upon the continual supervision of the artist. This, indeed, was what distinguished the firm from ordinary commercial enterprises. They may employ an artist to make designs, but they seldom employ him to supervise the execution of them. The result is that the designer usually produces what will suit the workman instead of the workman working to satisfy the artist. When execution and design are thus estranged, execution inevitably tends to deteriorate. For it is the spur of design, especially when the designer is himself the workman, that makes the workman do better than his former best. New tasks are set to him, as they are set to executants in music; and the artist at his elbow, or the artist in himself, urges him to perform them. But when the designer never sees the workman, and has no control over his work, his designs are often so unsuited to the material that the workmen get the habit of doing what they will with them. And in a purely commercial business the employer is content if the result sells well. He, being a man of business and probably knowing little about art, demands from artists designs which he thinks are likely to sell. He prefers an artist who follows the fashion to one who follows his own bent. We cannot blame him but only the public, which expects such a system to supply them with works of art.

Morris's aim was as far as possible to put an end to this estrangement between design and execution. He was determined that his design should be executed just as he wished; and further, he was determined to design as if he had the object designed already before him. He knew that an artist who designs in the abstract without any knowledge of his material can never follow his own bent, for it is knowledge of the material that provokes real invention in design. And he meant to follow his own bent

41. **Philip Webb**, *The Forest* (Detail), 1887.
Design for the tapestry *The Forest*.
Victoria & Albert Museum, London.

and then see if the public would not buy his goods. The taste consulted in the ordinary decorator's business is nobody's taste; it is merely what some businessman thinks may be the taste of the public. Morris meant to consult his own taste, for he knew that only by doing can an artist produce works of art.

The circular gave the following account of work that the firm proposed to do:

I.   Mural decoration, either in pictures or in pattern work, or merely in the arrangement of colours, as applied to dwelling houses, churches or public buildings.
II. Carving generally as applied to architecture.
III. Stained glass, especially with reference to its harmony with mural decoration.
IV. Metal work in all its branches, including jewellery.
V.   Furniture, either depending for its beauty on its own design, on the application of materials hitherto overlooked, or on its conjunction with figure and pattern painting.

Under this head is included embroidery of all kinds, stamped leather and ornamental work in other such materials, besides every article necessary for domestic use.

In this document, Mackail detects "the slashing hand and imperious accent of Rossetti," who never had any doubts about what he or any of his friends could do. But the wonder is that in course of time Morris did perform most of what was promised. Madox Brown and Burne-Jones designed stained glass and Webb, furniture. Albert Moore, William de Morgan and Simeon Solomon also helped. But Morris himself did the great mass of the designing, and he organised and supervised all the production. His way always was to set every one to work that he could lay hands on; and he had a wonderful power of making them do good work. Faulkner and his two sisters painted tiles and pottery; Mrs. Morris and her sister embroidered; and the foreman's wife helped to make altar-cloths. Premises were taken in Red Lion Square, Holborn, and the boys needed for the work were got from a boys' home. They were not chosen as possessing any special gifts, but many of them became good craftsmen under Morris. The first capital of the firm was £7 (£1 from each partner) and a loan of £100 from Morris's mother. The next year (1862) each partner contributed £19, and this capital was not increased until the dissolution of the partnership in 1874, though Morris and his mother lent a few hundred pounds more. Thus the finances of the firm were never well established or even defined; and its business was hampered until a capital grew out of the profits.

The firm is best known for its wallpapers and chintzes, and Morris began to design wallpapers as soon as it was founded. His first, the rose-trellis, was designed in 1862.

42. *The Forest*, 1887.

Tapestry. Woven wool and silk
on a cotton warp, 121.9 x 452 cm.
Victoria & Albert Museum, London.

The birds in it were drawn by Webb; for Morris, rightly or wrongly, thought that he could not draw animals and human beings well enough. Perhaps on this one point, he was lazy, for every one is lazy about something. Yet he used to draw from the model, as he said, "for his soul's good"; and he may have done that to cure his laziness. Certainly he had not that curiosity about form that loads a draughtsman like Rembrandt to pursue all the subtleties of form; just as in his writings he did not have the curiosity about character that led Shakespeare to draw Hamlet or Tolstoy to draw Levin. Rembrandt drew houses and trees as if they were human beings; but Morris was inclined to draw human beings as if they were flowers. He would start with a pattern in his mind and from the first saw everything as a factor in that pattern. But in these early wallpapers he showed a power of patternmaking that has never been equalled in modern times. For though everything is subject to the pattern, yet the pattern itself expresses a keen delight in the objects of which it is composed. So they are like poems in which the words keep a precise and homely sense and yet in their combination make music expressive of their sense. Others, perhaps, have shown an equal skill in spinning patterns; but their patterns have not seemed thus to grow naturally out of their subject matter. Morris never spoilt the beauty of his patterns by making them too pictorial; but they have a pictorial interest and their design seems as unforced and as appropriate as the composition of a good picture.

Yet Morris only applied his genius for design to wallpapers because, if his firm was to survive, he had to produce objects for which there was a demand. He knew that we have too many patterns in our houses and that all the arts of design have suffered from the ease with which patterns can be multiplied by mechanical processes. His own papers were printed by hand from wood blocks, and by that means were kept far closer to the original designs both in form and in colour than any mechanically printed papers could be. But even with hand-printing, whether of papers or of chintzes, a designer is not so much controlled and inspired by his material as when the execution of the design consists in a difficult manipulation of the material. Patterns are so easily produced by printing, even by hand-printing, on paper or linen, that the designer is tempted to think more of the beauty of his pattern than of the character of the material on which it is to be stamped. And Morris himself in his later work, when designing came easy to him from constant practice, produced patterns that are too abstract and elaborate. They cover a given space and repeat themselves with wonderful skill, but they have less character and sense than his earliest patterns. They are vastly superior to the many imitations of them, but they are not, like the rose-trellis or daisy papers, inimitable.

Even Morris suffered in his art from the evil conditions of his time, but he could not change them all at a stroke when he started his business. It has been supposed that his one aim was to do this, and he has been blamed for falling into compromise inconsistent with that aim. But he was an artist as well as a reformer of art, and he had the artist's proper and natural desire to practice his art, which he could only do

43. *The Woodpecker*, 1885.
   Tapestry.
   William Morris Gallery, London.

44. *Tulip and Willow*, 1873.
   Design. Pencil, watercolour and bodycolour,
   114.3 x 94 cm.
   Birmingham Museums and Art Gallery,
   Birmingham.

45. *Tulip and Willow*, 1873.
   Pattern for printed fabric, 135.5 x 93 cm.
   Victoria & Albert Museum, London.

I once a king and chief · now am the tree-barks thief :

ever twixt trunk and leaf · chasing the prey · ·

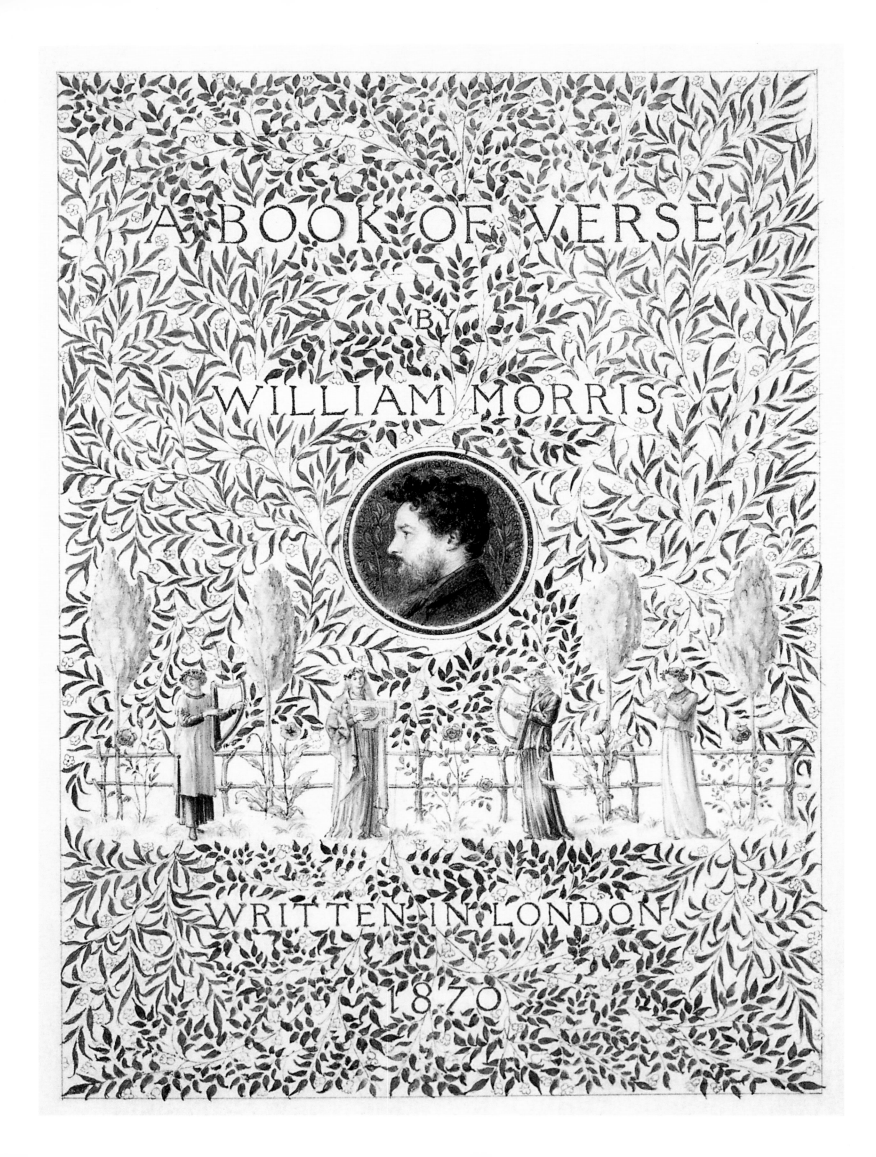

to any purpose by producing in answer to a demand. A painter nowadays might well think that mural painting was the highest and most rational form of his art. Believing that his art had suffered much through its complete divorce from decoration, he might make it the political object of his life to revive mural painting. Yet, if there were no walls for him to paint, he would not therefore give up painting altogether, but would paint easel pictures both to make a living and because he could not otherwise practice his art.

Because Morris was an artist and a reformer, he has been misjudged as both. If he had been only an artist, his art, in all its different forms, would have been accepted on its merits. Because he wished to change the conditions in which art is produced, he has been blamed for producing art subject to conditions as they are. But since he was an artist as well as a reformer, since, indeed, he only became a reformer because he was an artist, his problem as an artist was to do the best he could in existing conditions. Again, as a social reformer, he has been blamed because he produced expensive art for rich people. But, apart from the fact that when the firm was started, he had not yet become a social reformer, he had to produce art, if he was to produce it at all, for those who could buy it. He could not produce his art cheaply, because he had to learn, and to teach, most of the processes of its production. He revived art after art and process after process by his own private and personal efforts, and these efforts would have been futile if he had not found a market for his wares. He might have been reproached justly, perhaps, if he had made a great fortune by his labours; but he did not. The profits of the firm were for the most part used in extending its experiments. Morris himself was paid for his work; but the pay was less than a man of ordinary powers and ordinary industry could make as a barrister or a stockbroker; and Morris had powers and industry as great as those of any other man of his time. His aim, in founding his firm, was to do the work that he wished to do, not to obtain money or power. If he had wished to practice only the art of painting or of poetry, he could have done so alone and without any business organisation. But he wished to practice other arts in which he needed the help of fellow-artists and craftsmen; and, since these arts were costly to revive and practice, he needed a business organisation if he was to succeed with them. A painter need not keep his own shop; he can live by selling a few pictures a year and he can show them in galleries belonging to middlemen. But Morris, with his far greater and more diverse production and with his need for far greater sales, required a shop like any other tradesman. Indeed, he wished the artist to be a tradesman, as he was in Italy in the fifteenth century; and he saw no reason why the tradesman should not be an artist. He was both himself, and for that reason he had practical success which influenced the art of all Europe. Keats told Shelley that the artist must serve both God and Mammon, and Samuel Butler remarked that it is not easy to do that but that nothing worth doing ever is easy. Morris succeeded in doing it; but in the only way in which it can be done. That is to say, he served Mammon so that he might the better be able to serve God, and he was indifferent to the reproaches of those who serve neither.

46. *A Book of Verse*, 1870.

Front page.

Victoria & Albert Museum, London.

47. *Jasmine Trellis*, 1860.
Block printed on cotton, 22.9 x 94 cm,
pattern repeat, 45 x 45.5 cm.
Victoria & Albert Museum, London.

48. *Bird*, 1877-1878.
Design for woven textile.
Pencil and watercolour, 101.6 x 68.2 cm.
Inscribed with Queen Square address and
later address stamps.
William Morris Society, Kelmscott House, London.

Morris at the Red House was not only happy himself but the cause of happiness in others. Multitudes of friends visited him, among them Rossetti, Burne-Jones, Swinburne, Madox Brown, Philip Webb, and Arthur Hughes. They played bowls, and romped, and drove about the country in a leather-curtained carriage of Morris's own design. "It was the most beautiful sight in the world," says one of these friends, "to see Morris coming up from the cellar before dinner, beaming with joy, with his hands full of bottles of wine and others tucked under his arms." When his first daughter was christened in 1861, the house was so full that beds were strewn about the drawing room and Swinburne slept on a sofa. Faulkner remarks on Morris's tranquillity at this time: "I grieve to say he has only kicked one panel out of a door for this twelve month past."

Morris was one of those men who are chaffed the more they are admired and loved. His friends knew that he was a great man, but did not treat him as one. Indeed, he never gave himself the airs of a great man, and preferred companionship to admiration. No one resented his furies, because he himself laughed at them when they were over, and never used them to enforce his

predominance. He was intolerant of certain opinions; but when he flew into a rage it was the opinion that made him angry, not the person who expressed it. It cannot be said that he suffered fools gladly; but he had no cold contempt for them, and grew angry with trying to make them less foolish. One can see from the accounts of his friends that he forgot himself utterly in whatever he was doing at the moment; and it was, perhaps, the incongruity between their general idea of him and his appearance when absorbed in some trivial task, which made them laugh at him. Morris, coming up from the cellar with his hands and arms full of bottles, was the very picture of a jolly host out of Dickens. No one would have laughed at him if he had been nothing else. But he was the very picture of a hundred different things, great and small, in one day, and always unconsciously. So his friends laughed to see the essential Morris passing through all those changes and venting the same fury upon a door panel as upon a social iniquity. But they laughed because they were at ease in loving him.

This happy life did not last long. Morris fell ill of rheumatic fever, and after this illness was not strong enough to make the frequent journeys to London, which the

49. *Bird*, 1877-1878.
Hand-loom, jacquard-woven wollen double cloth, 304 x 182 cm.
Victoria & Albert Museum, London.

50. *Daisy*.
Hammersmith Terrace cloth.
Private collection.

growing business of the firm demanded. For this and other reasons he resolved to leave the Red House before he had finished decorating it. In 1865 he took an old house in Queen Square, Bloomsbury, and in the autumn he moved both his family and his business there, selling the Red House, which he never saw again. Living in London, he had more time to spare both because he was saved a long journey to his work and because he had found a good manager for his business. His choice

of manager was proof of his adventurous sagacity. George Warrington Taylor was a man of good family and education, who had lost all his money and fallen to be a check-taker at a theatre. Though he had mismanaged his own affairs, Morris set him to manage the business and it prospered steadily under him. Having thus more leisure, Morris turned to writing poetry again, and produced a prodigious amount in a short time. *The Life and Death of Jason* was published in 1867, the first and second parts of *The Earthly Paradise* together in 1868; the third and fourth separately in 1870. In spite of their length, all these volumes had a great and immediate success, and Morris from that time ranked with Rossetti and Swinburne as a chief of the new generation of Romantic poets. But even *The Earthly Paradise* did not end this burst of poetic energy, and in 1872 he wrote *Love is Enough*, the last of his longer romantic poems.

Morris as a Romantic Poet

The word Romantic, applied to a certain movement in art, has been used vaguely and in different senses. We know better who the Romantic poets are than why we call them Romantic. But if we examine their works, and especially those which any one would choose as being peculiarly romantic, we shall find that they have this in common – namely, that they interest us through their unlikeness, rather than through their likeness, to our own experience. In poems like Keats's *Eve of St Agnes* and *La Belle Dame sans Merci*, or like Coleridge's *Christabel* and *The Ancient Mariner*, there is a continual insistence upon the strangeness of the circumstances. It is not merely that the story belongs to the past; most stories told by poets do. But Homer and Chaucer do not incessantly remind us that their stories belong to the past, whereas Keats and Coleridge do. Homer and Chaucer tell a story because they think it a good one; but Coleridge in *Christabel* and Keats in the *Eve of St Agnes* have very little story to tell. The aim of these poems is to carry us into a strange world whose strangeness is more important

than what happens in it. Wordsworth, again, in his poems about peasants, though he does not carry us into the past, does transport us into a world different from our own, and he always insists upon the difference. Indeed, many of his incidents are chosen to illustrate the difference between his peasants and the people for whom he writes. In fact, the Romantic Movement expressed a general dissatisfaction with the circumstances and surroundings of the life of the Romantic poets.

It was not merely an attempt to enrich the subject matter of poetry or to deliver it from the prosaic methods of the eighteenth century. It was rather a revolt against the whole urban civilisation of that century, and the Romantic poets ranged the past because they were sick of the present. Some of them were liberal in their politics, others conservative, but Scott, the most conservative of them all, did not like the urban civilisation of his time well enough to write about it. He, too, not only found his stories in the past, but enjoyed it because it was unlike the present; and whenever he draws a character well from life it is a countryman sharply distinguished from the run of educated and well-to-do townspeople of the day. Shakespeare took Hamlet from a primitive Danish story and turned him into a gentleman of his own time. A Romantic poet would have made him even more primitive than he was in the original story; for he would have chosen that story as a way of escape from the present, and would have peopled it with strange, not with familiar, characters.

Now of all the Romantic poets, Morris, in his early poetry was the most romantic; for he was more consciously discontented with the circumstances of his own time than any of them. At the beginning of the Romantic Movement the Middle Ages had been discovered; that is to say, they had become interesting instead of being merely dull and barbarous. Horace Walpole built himself what he took to be a Gothic villa at Strawberry Hill, and wrote what he thought was a medieval romance in the *Castle of Otranto*. At first this interest in the Middle Ages was merely a new fashion, like the earlier fashion that produced Pastoral poetry, and it had results just as absurd. But it was a fashion that lasted, and people went on being interested in the Middle Ages without quite knowing why. To Keats and Coleridge they were full of a strange inexplicable beauty, well expressed in these lines from *Christabel*.

> The moon shines dim in the open air,
> And not a moonbeam enters here.
> But they without its light can see
> The chamber carved so curiously,
> Carved with figures strange and sweet,
> All made out of the carver's brain,
> For a lady's chamber meet:
> The lamp with twofold silver chain
> Is fastened to an angel's feet.

51. **Arthur Hughes**, *April Love*, 1855-1856.
    Oil on canvas, 89.9 x 49.5 cm.
    Tate Gallery, London.

52. **Dante Gabriel Rossetti**, *Proserpine*, 1874.
    Oil on canvas, 125.1 x 61 cm.
    Tate Gallery, London.

Then came Ruskin, who explained the causes and conditions of this beauty and why it could not be imitated now; and for Morris, who had learnt from Ruskin, and who studied the Middle Ages with the passion of an artist and of a man of science, their beauty was no longer fantastic or inexplicable. For him their art was as normal and rational as classical art seemed to the masters of the High Renaissance in Italy. It was the art of his own people and his own country, which had been for a time ousted by a foreign art, just as the southern art of Italy was for a time ousted by the Gothic.

But still it was not the art that he saw being produced about him. The tradition of it had been lost and would have to be recovered; and that could not be done by mere imitation. Meanwhile, however, he felt himself, as he said in the Introduction to *The Earthly Paradise*, to be born out of his due time. This feeling was not the result of a vague dislike of reality, but of a clear liking for a reality different from that in which he found himself. And in his first volume of poems we see him trying to throw himself back into that reality, and describing it as if it were something he remembered from his own childhood. The detail of poems such as *The Defence of Guenevere* or *King Arthur's Tomb* is not the vague detail of earlier poets. It is precise and described as if the poet were relating what he had seen with his own eyes. But he insists continually on it because he wishes not only to tell a story or express a passion, but also to describe a world different from that in which he lives. He is not entirely occupied with strange circumstance, for Guenevere and Lancelot and all the people of the *Morte d'Arthur* were real people to him; they were more real than the people he met in the street just because he thought of them as living in the world of his desires. So he could not bring them to life without also bringing that world to life. *The Defence of Guenevere* and *King Arthur's Tomb* are troubled and confused with this twofold task. In them Morris has too much to say; he is like a child trying to tell a story and at the same time expressing its own delighted interest in every detail of the story. He becomes both breathless and rambling in the effort. He is full of strange news about wonderful people in a wonderful world of his own discovery, and he tells it all as news, making no distinction of emphasis between one fact and another. Tennyson writes of the Court of King Arthur as if it were an old tale worth exploiting by a modern civilised poet. For him it is a story of no time or place; but for Morris it is a story of a time better than his own, not, of course, the real legendary time of King Arthur, but the Middle Ages still familiar to Mallory. And whereas Tennyson's treatment of circumstance is like the vague treatment of some idealist eighteenth-century painter, Morris reminds us of Mantegna in his mixture of living passion and detail drawn from the past. For Mantegna looked back to the Roman past just as Morris looked back to the past of the Middle Ages, and he too expressed his desire for another state of being in his art with a passion that freed his detail from pedantry.

The Defence of Guenevere contains one or two of Morris's earliest poems, such as the beautiful *Summer Dawn*, in which he seems to dream without energy. In the

53. **Arthur Hughes**, *The Eve of St Agnes*, 1856.
Oil on canvas, 71 x 124.5 cm.
Tate Gallery, London.

54. **John Everett Millais**, *Ophelia*, 1851-1852.
Oil on canvas, 76.2 x 111.8 cm.
Tate Gallery, London.

They told her how, upon St. Agnes' Eve,
Young virgins might have visions of delight,
And soft adorings from their loves receive
Upon the honey'd middle of the night,
If ceremonies due they did aright;
As, supperless to bed they must retire,
And couch supine their beauties, lily white;
Nor look behind, nor sideways, but require
Of Heaven with upward eyes for all that they desire.

later and medieval poems he is still dreaming, but with energy too fierce for a pure dreamer such as he still took himself to be. And it is this dreaming energy that makes those poems unlike other romantic poetry. The romantic game had been played in verse often enough, but here it is played in deadly earnest. Morris does not make use of the Middle Ages for artistic purposes; he writes about them as a poet writes of love when he is himself in love. In poems like *The Haystack in the Floods* we can see that he has taken his method from Browning. He tells a great deal of his story by means of allusion, and by the same means manages to introduce detail without labour or digression. But whereas Browning used this method to express his curiosity about many past ages, Morris used it to express his passion for one. He writes not like a curious traveler through all the past, but like one who has traveled to find what he wants and has found it. No one, perhaps, could see at the time that there was more than dreaming in those poems, but we can see now that they were written by a man who would try to make his dreams come true.

In *The Defence of Guenevere* volume there is one poem, *Sir Peter Harpdon's End*, in blank verse and dramatic in form. After the publication of that volume Morris began writing, also dramatic and in blank verse, a series of *Scenes from the Fall of Troy*. He never finished them, partly because at the time he was too busy with the firm and partly because his mind was being drawn more and more to narrative. It was contrary to his practical nature to write drama that was not completely a play and that was not meant to be acted. He showed in these experiments that he had more dramatic power than most modern poets, both in his invention and in the style of his blank verse, which is poetry yet sounds like natural speech; but he never developed this dramatic power for want of a theatre and actors. The tale of Troy, like the tale of King Arthur, was to him a story of the Middle Ages, but one which the Middle Ages had got from a past already far remote. He saw it, whereas most modern writers only think of it; but he saw it faint in an infinite distance and through a transforming mist. He always felt the sadness *"of old unhappy far-off things and battles long ago,"* but this sadness is heavier in the Troy scenes than in any of his other work. The people all seem like ghosts, acting their past faintly over again with a foreknowledge of its futile end. It is as if he had evoked them and then soon dismissed them out of pity; but in these fragments there is a real evocation and, however pale the ghosts may be, we believe at least that they are ghosts.

After this Morris wrote little verse for six or seven years, and when he began again in London he made no more experiments. Then he set to work upon narrative poetry, knowing exactly what he meant to do and well able to do it. He was lucky in that he had a great natural talent for a kind of poetry that has not often been written well in England. Since the *Canterbury Tales,* most of our poetical narrative poems have not told a story well; and most that have told a story well have been either prosaic or poetic only by artifice. Morris told his stories naturally in verse

55. *Vineyard*, 1873-1874.

Design. Pencil and watercolour,

81.4 x 64.6 cm.

Victoria & Albert Museum, London.

because he could conceive them as poems; and at this time he was content to be a poetic teller of old stories. Chaucer was his master in this art and from him he seems to have learnt, without practice on his own account, all that can be learnt of it; and in particular how to make the poetry issue naturally out of the story instead of using the story as a pretext for irrelevant poetry. And, like Chaucer in the *Canterbury Tales,* Morris in his *Earthly Paradise* devises circumstances that provide a plausible reason for storytelling. But, whereas Chaucer's pilgrims tell stories fitted to their own individual characters, the narrators of *The Earthly Paradise* each tell a story of his own race or country. Since, then, his stories were half Greek and half from other sources, he had to contrive a setting in which Greeks surviving from the ancient world meet with men of the Middle Ages and of many different countries. Hence the Prologue, a fine story in itself, in which, in the time of Edward III, a crew of sailors set out to find the Earthly Paradise, and after many adventures and disappointments come to an island where there are Greeks still living their old way of life, unknown to the rest of mankind. Thus this great exchange of tales is made possible.

But Morris, for all his love of a story, could not tell one as Chaucer could. Chaucer often thought he was relating history and, like a good historian, put all his knowledge of living men into it. Morris knew that he was simply telling stories, and in *The Earthly Paradise* he tells most of them as if he knew they were mere stories and as if he were passing them on as best he could. He set himself a task and performed it at a great pace. But no man who ever lived could tell all these diverse stories so as to express his own experience through them. When he wrote *The Earthly Paradise,* Morris still had the romantic conception of poetry, namely, that it should interest by its unlikeness rather than by its likeness to our experience. Therefore he lays his stress upon the wonderful events in his tales and upon their strangeness of circumstance rather than upon those passions and characters that are constant to men. It is events and circumstances that we remember rather than people. The poetry of *The Earthly Paradise* has been rather foolishly compared to the design of his wall-papers and chintzes; but it is true that Morris often gives as faint an image of reality in a story as in a pattern, and that he relies on the story, as on the pattern, to justify the faintness. No modern English poet had written a long poem of any kind so easy to read. Begin one of the tales of *The Earthly Paradise* and you find that it draws you along with its own current. Begin Swinburne's *Tristram,* and you find that after each splendid lyrical passage you have to set yourself to the story with an effort. All the best of it is digression; but there are no digressions in *The Man Born to be King,* and, as it is all poetry, this is high praise. But I, for one, can never feel quite satisfied with *The Earthly Paradise* and I even feel that its popularity has injured Morris's fame. A great deal of it is merely pleasure-giving poetry, and if he had written nothing else he would indeed have been the idle singer of an empty day. Perhaps, being at this time a little bewildered by life and the stale of the world, seeing that things were wrong and not having got any clear determination to right them, he set himself a task and

56. *Burnet*, 1881.

Wallpaper.

Victoria & Albert Museum, London.

tried to satisfy his enormous energy with that. He liked to think of poetry as a craft; and he had mastered the craft of storytelling so that it was almost too easy to him, and so that he could practice it without giving the whole of his mind to it. Indeed, one feels a kind of absence of mind in many of these stories, as if the writer knew them so well that he could think of something else while he was telling them; and for that reason he often seems to be telling us something to amuse us rather than because he must tell it.

He had meant *The Life and Death of Jason* to be part of *The Earthly Paradise*; but as he wrote it, it grew too large to take its place there. It is a poem of pure romance, told for its wonder and very well told; until near the end when Medea, from having been only a wonderful enchantress, becomes a mother, and has to subdue the tenderness common to all mothers before she can slay her children. Then Morris surprises us with a power like Chaucer's of expressing passion in the simplest words. This same power is demonstrated in *The Lovers of Gudrun*, which comes at the end of the third part of *The Earthly Paradise*. Two years before it was published Morris had begun to learn Icelandic, and he soon read through most of the sagas. He enjoyed all good stories; but these were to him among the stories of the world what Gothic was among all the different kinds of architecture; and he put the whole force of his mind into *The Lovers of Gudrun*, telling it not merely for its strangeness, but because he loved the men and women in it. But of this change in his poetry I will speak in another chapter. Two years after *The Earthly Paradise* was finished he made another dramatic experiment. *Love is Enough* is more remote from reality than any of his poems. Mackail has given a lucid account of its peculiar form with its receding planes of action, five in all, whose aim, starting from a representation of the outer world and particular persons, is to reach in the furthest plane an expression, almost in pure music, of that passion possessing the chief character of the play. For success in such a design, a sharp contrast would be needed between the nearer and the more distant planes; and the contrast in the poem is not sharp. The rustics in the nearest plane are as faint as any persons in *The Earthly Paradise* and all the other characters are shadows, so that the lyrics of the furthest plane seem nearer to us than anything else in the poem. *Love is Enough* seems a shadowy romance, but it is really a religious play, a confession of faith made almost unconsciously.

The love of which the lyrics tell is not the love of one human being for another, though that may be a preparation for it. It is rather a state of mind that, to those who know it, is better than happiness, indeed the best that man can attain to in this life.

But Morris can express it better than I can explain it:

> "Ye know not how void is your hope and your living:
> Depart with your helping lest yet ye undo me.

57. **Morris, Marshall, Faulkner & Co.**
(for the publication) and **Jeffrey & Co.**
(for the production), *Chrisanthemum*, 1877.
Wallpaper. Wood block colour prints.
Victoria & Albert Museum, London.

> Ye know not that at nightfall she draweth near to me,
> There is soft speech between us and words of forgiving,
> Till in dead of the midnight her kisses thrill through me.
> Pass by me, and hearken, and waken me not."

This language is recognised at once by any one who has an ear for it. It is the language of religious ecstasy, expressing a desire so strong that it can use the terms of earthly love, and so sweet to those who feel it that it has in it also the delight of earthly love.

Morris, like all great men of his kind, was unworldly, not so much from contempt of the world, certainly not from contempt of the earth, as because there was something desired by his soul compared with which things of the world seemed to him of little account. As a rule he acted upon this desire more than he thought about it. He was not by nature speculative, and shared the skepticism of his time about all supernatural things. He set himself so many tasks that he was more concerned with performing them than with asking himself why he did so. But sometimes that high passion, which was the motive force of his life, expressed itself suddenly in his poetry so that it seems to tell a secret of which he was hardly aware himself, a secret only to be understood by those who know it already. In ordinary speech Morris, though very frank, told no secrets about himself; and all his friends knew that there was a part of him that he shared with no one. Here he reveals it in his art, telling all the world that there is a source outside him from which he gets his strength and purpose; and then he turns proudly on the world as if he had told it too much:

> Wherewith will ye buy it, ye rich who behold me?
> Draw out from your coffers your rest and your laughter,
> And the fair gilded hope of the dawn coming after.
> Nay, this I sell not – though ye bought me and sold me –
> For your house stored with such things from threshold to rafter,
> Pass by me. I hearken, and think of you not.

When he wrote this he was still, like an eremite, half afraid of the world, and withdrawing from it to listen to the whispers of his familiar. But these very whispers were to send him into the world again so that he might labour to change what he hated.

Love is Enough is half a failure as a romantic poem because Morris could no longer soothe his disgust of reality by writing of strange things. The romantic part of it persists from mere habit and has become as faint as a fading memory. Indeed, the music of the lyrics makes us forget it altogether, and they break through it as if the poet himself had forgotten it. In them we hear no longer the idle singer of an empty day but one whose music is making itself out of his own experience.

58. *Spring*, 1873.
   One of four panels of stained glass in the Inglenook fireplace in the Dining Room of Cragside. Northumberland.

A Flowering Career

The Revival of Arts and Crafts

For some years Morris was mainly occupied with his different arts and his business, and still tried to live like an artist unconcerned with other matters. In 1871 he took with Rossetti a beautiful old house on the Upper Thames called Kelmscott Manor House, which he has described in *News from Nowhere*. He meant it to be a happy refuge from the world; but the contrast between it and most houses of our own time, especially the houses of the poor, troubled him more and more, so that he could not rest content with its bygone excellence. More and more, as he lived there, the quiet waters of the river at his garden end drew his thoughts with them down to the city in which the present was making so blind a preparation for the future:

Hark, the wind in the elm-boughs! From London it bloweth,
And telleth of gold, and of hope and unrest;
Of power that helps not, of wisdom that knoweth,
But teacheth not aught of the worst and the best.

So he wrote at a later time when, go where he would, he could not escape from the noise of London and the questions it put to him. At this time he wrote now and again about the state of society as if it were a matter that troubled him through his work like a distracting noise that could not be stopped. He says, in a letter written in 1874:

"It seems to be nobody's business, to try to do better things – isn't mine, you see, in spite of all my grumbling – but look, suppose people lived in little communities among gardens and green fields, so that they could be in the country in five minutes' walk, and had few wants, almost no furniture, for instance, and no servants, and studied the (difficult) arts of enjoying life, and finding out what they really wanted; then I think we might hope civilisation had really begun."

He had already a clear notion of the way of life which seemed to him best for the whole of society; and in this he was unlike many revolutionaries whose aim is to change the machinery of society without having ever asked themselves what they want to do with it when they have changed it. But the machinery itself puzzled Morris so that he was not anxious to start meddling with it. After *Love is Enough*, he wrote nothing original for some time. "Sometimes," he wrote in a letter, "I begin to fear I am losing my invention. You know I very much wish not to fall off in imagination and enthusiasm as I grow older." Yet the best of his life both in action and in literature was yet to be; and the slack time only meant that he was being pulled different ways. It would not have been a slack time for any one else. He went on translating sagas, and in 1875 he published a translation of Virgil's *The Aeneid*.

59. **Edward Burne-Jones** (for the design) and **Morris, Marshall, Faulkner & Co.** (for the production), *Painting*, 1862. Stained glass panels of the series *King Rene's Honeymoon*, 64.5 x 54.8 x 3.2 cm. Victoria & Albert Museum, London.

In this work, because of the merits and defects of the original, Morris showed clearly what were his own shortcomings in poetry. *The Aeneid*, though a narrative poem, was not written for the story and is not read for it. It has every merit except that momentum which only a great story-teller can give to narrative. The mind of the reader rests on the beautiful passages and is not drawn through them by a desire to discover what will happen next. Virgil is a poet who broods over his theme; thought, not action, is the stuff of his poetry; and his language, though not obscure, is complicated and enriched with thought. But Morris was a story-teller by nature, and his language, compared with Virgil's, is thin and quick and fluent. So when he translated the *The Aeneid*, he rendered it too closely to make a good story of it, while he could find no equivalent in his own language for the profound and subtle beauties of the original. Mackail says that he turned the *The Aeneid* into a romantic poem; it seems to me that he tried to turn it into a purely narrative poem and failed, as he would have failed with *Paradise Lost*, if it had been written in a foreign tongue and he had translated it into English. Morris's translation can be read with pleasure; but it is like some of the vaguer stories of *The Earthly Paradise*, and the *The Aeneid* is not like these at all.

In 1875 the partnership of Morris & Co. was dissolved, and Morris's friendship with Rossetti came to an end. There was a dispute about the terms of dissolution between Morris on the one hand and Rossetti, Madox Brown and Marshall on the other. Morris made friends again with Brown, but never with Rossetti, who was sick in mind and body. But this dispute about the firm was only the final occasion of their quarrel. Morris had once been Rossetti's happy slave; now he was his equal with different desires and different values. He wrote in a letter after Rossetti's death:

"I can't say, how it was that Rossetti took no interest in politics... The truth is he cared for nothing but individual and personal matters; chiefly of course in relation to art and literature; but he would take abundant trouble to help any one person who was in distress of mind or body; but the evils of any mass of people he couldn't bring his mind to bear upon. I suppose, in short, it needs a person of hopeful mind to take disinterested notice of politics, and Rossetti was certainly not hopeful."

60. **Ford Maddox Brown** (for the design) and **Morris, Marshall, Faulkner & Co.** (for the production), *Architecture*, c. 1863. Stained glass panels of the series *King Rene's Honeymoon*, 64.5 x 54.8 x 3.2 cm. Victoria & Albert Museum, London.

Here Morris states very clearly the difference between Rossetti and himself. For he himself was always more concerned about general evils than about the troubles of individuals, and in that respect he belonged peculiarly to his own age. People often talk of Morris as if he was a man of the Middle Ages, born, as he said himself, out of due time. But the very comparisons, which he made between one age and another, would never have been made by any medieval mind. He saw past and present in the mass, and he saw individual things as symptoms of a general state of being. This tendency of his mind is the modern scientific tendency, the power of which we may judge from the fact that it became a habit in one who was so little interested in science. Morris might have been a greater artist if he had been more passionately concerned with particular people and things, if they had not all seemed to him representative of certain conceptions in his own mind. For even his energy, and with it his interests, had limits. He understood types of character well, and could draw them firmly and justly; nor was he at all a doctrinaire in his judgments of men and things. But they remained generic for him, and in his art he presents them as typical of what he likes and dislikes. As an artist, in fact, he is a generaliser of a new kind; for he uses his generalisations to express likes and dislikes that are not merely instinctive but also the result of his general conceptions of what is good and bad. And yet he differs from all those who have employed art for ulterior ends, who have written novels with a purpose, or pictures with a moral, in that art is for him always simply a means of expression. He does not try to prove anything by it any more than Shakespeare or Rembrandt; but, unlike them, he expresses an interest, a peculiarly modern interest, in states of being rather than in men and women.

But the scientific tendency affected him in another and more definite way; for it made him an eager inquirer into methods and processes of art. He soon became aware that many of the arts and crafts which he practiced were in the dark ages of ignorance; and he made it his business to recover past knowledge about them as eagerly as the men of the Renaissance tried to recover the knowledge of the ancient world. Dyeing was one of these arts; for he found that, when he had designed a pattern, its colours could not be reproduced with the dyes of the time, and further that, until he himself had some knowledge of dyeing, he could not design dyed stuffs with any freedom or precision of invention. At first he did the best he could with things as they were. His foreman, Mr. George Wardle says:

"His skill as a colourist was shown in combining colours which, separately, were of but very mediocre character. This system of colour, which may be called provisional, marks very distinctly what may be called the first period of the history of the firm, when Mr. Morris had not yet got a dye-house. The peacock-blues, rusty reds, and olive-greens of that period were not by any means his ideals, but the best he could get done."

The colours of this provisional period became fashionable, and were thought peculiarly artistic by people of timid taste. Indeed, they still persist as "art" colours, but Morris himself was soon sick of them and of the reputation they brought him. Once when a customer, shocked by the brightness of the later Hammersmith carpets, remarked, "But I thought your colours were subdued?" Morris dealt with him firmly: "If you want dirt," he said, "you can find that in the street."

61. **Dante Gabriel Rossetti** (for the design) and **Morris, Marshall, Faulkner & Co.** (for the production), *Music*, c. 1863. Stained glass panels of the series *King Rene's Honeymoon*, 64.5 x 54.8 x 3.2 cm. Victoria & Albert Museum, London.

62. *The Annunciation*, 1861.

Stained glass window.

All Saints Church, Selsey, Gloucestershire.

the lord is with thee

Before he had his own dye-house he was continually disappointed by the bad work of those he employed to dye for him both in England and in France. But he could not set up his own dye-house until he had taught himself to dye; and he had to learn the secrets of vegetable-dyeing mainly from old books, for there were few living men who knew anything about it. He studied French works of the sixteenth and seventeenth centuries, Herbals, and even Philemon Holland's translation of Pliny, as ardently as if he were Browning's Grammarian labouring at the Greek language. "I was at Kelmscott the other day," he writes in 1870, "and betwixt the fishing, I cut, a handful of poplar twigs and boiled them, and dyed a lock of wool a very good yellow." He had the power of understanding what he read in books so well that he could put it in practice at once. He made his first experiments with his own hands and "so well had he prepared himself," says Mr. Wardle, "that I do not think a single dyeing went wrong." He also learnt what he could from Mr. Thomas Wardle, the brother of his foreman, who was a practical dyer at Leek and who remembered something of the old vegetable dyeing as it was practiced in his own boyhood. It was at Leek that he revived indigo dyeing, which, because of its difficulty, had been superseded by Prussian blue. "It requires," he said "more experience than any dyeing process," and for that reason, and because no substitute could satisfy him, he worked at it as if he had nothing else in the world to do. "I must say I should like not to look such a beast," he wrote after dyeing in the indigo Tat, "and not to feel as if I wanted pegs to keep my fingers one from the other."

But dyeing was only one of the arts that he revived by the simple but arduous process of learning how to practice them himself. He was for a time hampered by want of space; but in 1881 he moved his works from London to Merton Abbey. There he found some disused print-works close to the River Wandle, the water of which was suitable to his dyeing, and with the works seven acres of land including a meadow, an orchard, and a garden.

Here is a list of the different kinds of work executed at Merton Abbey, which Mackail gives in his Life:

1. Painted glass windows.
2. Arras tapestry woven in the high-warp loom.
3. Carpets.
4. Embroidery.
5. Tiles.
6. Furniture.
7. General house decoration.
8. Printed cotton goods.
9. Paper-hangings.
10. Figured woven stuffs.
11. Velvets and cloths.
12. Upholstery.

63. **Edward Burne-Jones** and **John Henry Dearle**, *Justice, Courage, Humility and Angels*, c. 1897. Watercolour and ink, 23.5 x 15.6 cm. Sketch design for the east window of St Mary the Virgin, Godmanchester, Huntingdonshire. Private collection.

Haywards Heath

East Window
St. Wilfred's Cuckfield
14 June 1867

The Property of
Morris Company
26 Queen Square
Bloomsbury. London

64. **John Henry Dearle,**
Reunion in Paradise, Christ Savior and the Three Archangels Surrounded by the Celestial Court.
Sketch for the Rugby School Chapel.
Watercolour and ink.
Private collection.

65. **Edward Burne-Jones** and **Philip Webb** (designers) for **Morris, Marshall, Faulkner & Co.,**
The Virgin Mary, Christ on the Cross, St John, the Adoration of the Magi, the Nativity, the Adoration of the Shepherds, the Annunciation and the Holy Spirit, 1867.
Sketch design for the east window of St Wilfrid's, Haywards Heath, Sussex.
Watercolour and ink, 31.1 x 15.2 cm.
Private collection.

How Tristram & Isoude were buried together in one tomb in Cornwall : Now Tristram invented all manner of words that they use in hunting and the writing of notes in music : He was a mighty hunter & a great minstrel

For most of those Morris made designs himself and at Merton he was able to watch over the execution of all of them. His revival of tapestry was one of his last commercial ventures, and he was drawn into it simply by his love of the beautiful tapestries of the Middle Ages. Tapestries have been woven both on the high-warp and on the low-warp loom for thousands of years; and they are still woven on the high-warp loom at the Gobelins works where Morris went to see the process. But there, though the process was right enough, it was employed merely to make copies of paintings, so that all the beauties peculiar to tapestry were lost in the vain imitation of another art. Morris wished to revive not only the right process, extinct in England, but also the right principles of design. And to do this it was necessary for him to understand thoroughly the process for which the design was to be made, to be both artist and craftsman himself. Only the high-warp process could content him; for with the low-warp, where the frames are placed horizontally with the ground, the face of the tapestry looks downwards and the workman only sees the back of it. Thus he can only copy his design mechanically, matching colours as close as he can get them. But with the high-warp loom the frame stands vertically and the front of the tapestry is reflected to the workman in a mirror, so that he sees what he is doing and can translate his design into tapestry, making the picture in the material and suiting it to all the qualities of the material. In 1878 Morris began to think of practicing the art, and he said that whatever he did he must do chiefly with his own hands. "Tapestry at its highest," he said, "is the painting of pictures with coloured wools on a warp. Nobody but an artist can paint pictures." It was in the same year that he went to live in Hammersmith in a house so close to the river, that he could go by water from it to his other house at Kelmscott. There he had a tapestry loom set up in his bedroom and could work upon it for hours before breakfast. Sometimes he would give ten hours a day to it, and even when at Kelmscott he longed to get back to his weaving.

Having learnt all he could at home, he set up a loom at his works at Queen Square. Then he began to teach what he knew to his workmen, and he found that boys learnt most easily. Three of them were taught at Queen Square, and, though chosen almost at random, they soon became expert and carried on the work on a larger scale in the greater space at Merton, where the finest tapestries of modern times were produced, many of them, such as the *Adoration of the Magi*, from designs by Burne-Jones. In many of these tapestries the workman himself invented most of the colour and a good deal of the detail; this would have been impossible with the low-warp tapestry in which the workman, since he cannot see his work, must be a mere copyist. Thus, while designers like Burne-Jones and craftsmen like Dearle, who was the first boy trained by Morris, all played a great part in the revival of the art of tapestry weaving, they would never have had a chance of accomplishing anything in the field had Morris not first taught himself what he afterwards taught to others. All his fertility of design – and he designed nearly six hundred patterns of different kinds – would have been useless if he had not brought the artist and the craftsman once more together in his own person. It was he who discovered that to separate them is to deprive the artist of his art and the craftsman of his craft; and, having discovered the disease, he proceeded

66. **Edward Burne-Jones,**
The Tomb of Tristan and Iseult the Fair from *The Story of Tristan and Iseult.*
Stained glass window from the Music Room, Harden Grange.
Bradford Art Galleries and Museums, West Yorkshire.

C.323-1927

at once to prove, by his own example, the cure. This alone would have been a great work for one man's life, even if he had revived a single art; Morris, besides all his other labours, went on from one art to another. It was many years later that he took up the art of printing, but I may as well speak here of what he did for it.

It may be said that the art of printing began to decline soon after it was first established. The earliest printed books are the finest because their type was based upon beautiful writing, as it was practiced when calligraphy was an art. Printing killed calligraphy and soon began to suffer from the death of that art. There was beautiful type, of course, for many generations, but by the middle of the nineteenth century it had ceased to exist, and there was merely commercial printing as we have it today, ugly, mean, and not easily readable. Morris did not like his own books to be printed in this way, and in 1888 he resolved to do something better with his prose romance, *The House of the Wolfings*. He consulted his friend Emery Walker, and they chose a type about fifty years old, belonging to Mrs. Whittingham, which was modelled on an old Basel fount. He used the same type for *The Roots of the Mountains*, published in 1889, and the next year he resolved to set up a printing press of his own with type designed by himself. He was himself a calligraphist, and the writing of his illuminated manuscripts, if not as skilful as that of the great illuminators, was both beautiful and original. Like the first designers of type, he could therefore design with the art of the calligraphist, and he explained his aims in a note upon the Kelmscott Press. "I have always been a great admirer," he says, "of the calligraphy of the Middle Ages and of the earlier printing which took its place." It was the essence of his undertaking, he added, to produce books which it would be a pleasure to look upon as pieces of printing and arrangement of type; and he had to consider chiefly the following things: the paper, the form of the type, the relative spacing of the letters, the words, and the lines; and lastly the position of the printed matter on the page.

As to the type, he wanted "letter pure in form, severe, without needless excrescences, solid, without the thickening and thinning of the lino, which is the essential fault of the ordinary modern type, and which makes it difficult to read; and not compressed laterally as all later type has grown to be owing to commercial exigencies." His models for this kind of type were "the works of the great Venetian printers of the fifteenth century, of whom Nicholas Jenson produced the most complete and most Roman characters from 1470 to 1480." This type, he tells us, he studied with much care, "getting it photographed to a big scale, and drawing it over many times before I began designing my own letter; so that, though I think I mastered the essence of it, I did not copy it servilely."

So he made his first type, Roman in character, which is called Golden type. Miss May Morris tells us that he used to carry about with him proofs of the type in matchboxes and that sometimes, as he sat and talked, he would draw a matchbox out and thoughtfully eye the small scraps of paper inside it. He said that of all the designing he had ever done, nothing had ever given him so much trouble as this Roman type; and yet any one looking

67. **Edward Burne-Jones** (for the design) and **Morris, Marshall, Faulkner & Co.** (for the production), *The Prince*, c. 1860. Stained and painted glass, 33.6 x 18.4 cm. Victoria & Albert Museum, London.

68. **Edward Burne-Jones** (for the design) and **Morris, Marshall, Faulkner & Co.** (for the production), *Merchant's Daughter*, c. 1860. Stained and painted glass, 33.6 x 18.4 cm. Victoria & Albert Museum, London.

69. **Edward Burne-Jones** (for the design) and **Morris, Marshall, Faulkner & Co.** (for the production), *Sculpture*, 1862. Stained glass panels of the series *King Rene's Honeymoon*, 64.5 x 54.8 x 3.2 cm. Victoria & Albert Museum, London.

111

at it who knew nothing about type would only notice that it was easy to read and pleasant to the eye. It has no archaic peculiarities; indeed, there is more common sense in it, perhaps, than in any of the fine modern types that have since been produced.

"After a while," Morris says in his note, "I felt that I must have a Gothic as well as a Roman font; and herein the task I set myself was to redeem the Gothic character from the charge of unclearness that is commonly brought against it." So, he continues, "I designed a black-letter type which, I think, I may claim to be as readable as a Roman one, and to tell the truth, I prefer it to the Roman." This Gothic type in its larger form was called the Troy type. His Chaucer, with its double columns, was printed in a smaller form called the Chaucer type.

Morris was so used to black lettering, and so fond of it, that it gave no trouble to his eye. He felt that he must have a Gothic font, no doubt because of his love of everything Gothic. And yet even the finest Gothic lettering is neither so beautiful nor so rational as the lettering, which we may call Romanesque, of earlier manuscripts. In this matter Morris followed his own private taste and was a little whimsical; but at any rate he made his type as readable as any Gothic could be. It has not had as much influence on printing as his Roman type; but he pleased himself with it, and, in the larger form especially, it is beautiful.

The few details I have given show what pains Morris was ready to take with any art, and how humbly he learnt from past masters. He took just as much pain over everything connected with the press, especially with paper; and in everything he had the help of Emery Walker, without whom Miss May Morris tells us, the press could not have existed. Through all the later years of his life, from 1891 until the end, he gave more attention to printing than to any other art; and this fact proves how practical he was in all his artistic projects. For, since more books are read now than ever before, there is no art more constantly practiced than that of printing. But we are so little used to associate the arts with our common needs and habits that we do not regard it as an art at all. Pictures are art and poetry is art, but the type in which poetry is printed is, for most of us, merely a means of multiplying copies of it. There are many rich people who would give thousands of pounds for a picture, but who would never think of giving even one pound for a well printed edition of a favourite poet. They have not learnt to look for pleasure in type; and yet there is a beauty in a well printed page which, when it is once seen, will heighten the beauty of any verse or prose. Morris felt this beauty when hardly any one else did, and he was drawn to fine printing just because it added the beauty of art to a useful process. He could not endure a badly printed book as tidy people cannot endure untidiness. It was to him something badly done that might be well done, something like poor speech or bad grammar. Therefore, since there was no good printing in his time, he set to work to print well himself. And by doing so he opened the eyes of many people to the beauty of good printing, and created a demand for it which continues and which, we may hope, will increase. And so it was with all the arts that he revived or reformed. Ruskin had been the first

70. **Edward Burne-Jones** (for the design) and **Morris, Marshall, Faulkner & Co.** (for the production), *The God of Love and Alceste*, 1861-1864. Stained glass window from Chaucer's *Goode Wimmen*, 46.8 x 50.7 cm. Victoria & Albert Museum, London.

71. **Edward Burne-Jones** (for the design) and **Morris & Co.** (for the production), *Gawain and the Quest for the Holy Grail*, 1885-1886. Stained glass window, 46 x 33 cm. Victoria & Albert Museum, London.

72. **Edward Burne-Jones** (for the design) and **Morris & Co.** (for the production), *Lancelot and the Quest for the Holy Grail*, 1885-1886. Stained glass window, 46 x 33 cm. Victoria & Albert Museum, London.

how gawaine sought the sangreal and might not see it
because his eyes were blinded by thoughts of the deeds of kings

how lancelot sought the sangreal and might not see it because his eyes were blinded by such love as dwelleth in kings' houses

scientific critic. He had shown what were the causes of tightness in art and what were the causes of wrongness. He had done his best to deliver men from that paralysing belief, afterwards so vivaciously expressed by Whistler, that "art happens." Art does not happen, he contended, any more than good government happens. Like anything else, it is something that may be done well or badly. Morris put this doctrine to practice. Seeing many arts about him badly done, he set to work to discover how they could be done well, and he learnt from the past just as a wise statesman will learn from other nations. He knew that talent in the individual artist cannot be secured, but that a right method can, and in every art that he practiced he laboured to discover the right method, seeing that, when such was discovered, men of talent would use it and so make the most of their powers. The common notion is that the arts will be best encouraged by the discovery and patronage of men of talent. Morris never looked about for these. He taught himself an art and then taught it to any man or boy who was willing to learn. He knew from his study of the arts of the past that their well being depended not on the chance appearance of a few men of genius, but on the proper training of the ordinary workman. And that, in its turn, depended upon the public demand for good work. Therefore he tried to make a public demand for good work by producing it. And it was his effort, and the manner in which he found it constantly hampered by the social conditions of his time, which led him from art into polities. He, as an artist and a workman, judged the social conditions of his time and found them wanting, and just as he had set to work to improve the practice of the arts, so he set to work, no less simply, to improve social conditions.

The Sagas and "Sigurd"

In 1860, so that he might read the sagas in the original, Morris began learning Icelandic with Eirík Magnússon as his teacher. The following year he was already translating sagas with Magnússon. We can best understand why he loved them more than any other literature in the world from a statement he made years later regarding the Norsemens' religion:

> "It may be that the world shall worsen, that men shall grow afraid to 'change their lives,' that the world shall be weary of itself and sicken, and none but faint hearts be left – who knows? So at any rate comes the end at last, and the evil, bound for a while, is loose, and all nameless merciless horrors that on earth we figure by fire and earthquake and venom and ravin. So comes the great strife, and like the kings and heroes that they have loved, here also must the gods die, the gods who made that strifeful imperfect earth, not blindly indeed, yet foredoomed. One by one they extinguish for ever some dread and misery that all this time has brooded over life, and one by one, their work accomplished, they die: till at last the great destruction breaks out over all things, and the old earth and heavens are gone, and then a new heaven and earth. What goes on there? Who shall say, of us who know only of rest and

73. *Minstrel*, 1872-1874.
Stained and painted glass, 71 x 43 cm.
Victoria & Albert Museum, London.

117

MAGNUS ARTURUS REX
POTENTISSIMUS ANGLIAE

OMINUS L·UNCELOT DU LAC
QUES INVICTUS

74. *King Arthur and Sir Lancelot*, 1862.
Stained glass window.
Bradford Art Galleries and Museums,
West Yorkshire.

peace by toil and strife? And what shall be our share in it? Well, sometimes we must think that we shall live again. Yet if that were not, would it not be enough that we helped to make this unnameable glory, and lived not altogether deedless? Think of the joy we have in praising great men, and how we turn their stories over and over, and fashion their lives for our joy. And this also we ourselves may give to the world."

To this statement of the northern faith he adds: "I think one would be a happy man if one could hold it, in spite of the wild dreams and dreadful imaginings that hang about it now and then." We may wonder how a man so fortunate, with such a capacity for happiness and such an experience of it, could wish for such a faith as this; but in some verses to a saga-teller he lets us know:

Tale-teller, who 'twixt fire and sword
And heart to turn about and show
With faint half-smile things great and small
That in thy fearful land did fall,
Thou and thy brethren sure did gain
That thing for which I long in vain,
The spell, whereby the mist of fear
Was melted, and your ears might hear
Earth's voices as they are indeed.
Well ye have helped me at my need.

Here and elsewhere Morris tells us that, brave as he was, he suffered from that fear which darkens all skeptical and artificial societies, a fear so general that it becomes a mood and often can hardly name its object. It may be a fear of death, or of the sudden breakdown of the delicate machinery of civilisation, or of something sinister in the whole order of the universe. Fierce materialism, the determined belief that everything we take an emotional joy in is illusion, is only a courageous form of it. But whatever form it takes, the more men labour and contrive for their own security, the more it haunts them. But in the sagas Morris read of men who, with no kind of security, were free from that fear. Courage, not merely in particular actions, but as a state of mind, courage in facing the unknown as well as the known, was their chief virtue; and it shows itself not only in the deeds of which the sagas tell but also in their manner of telling them. This courage Morris himself desired so much that he was ready to sacrifice everything for it and for the art which seemed to him a symptom of it.

"Perhaps," he said, "the gods are preparing troubles and terrors for the world (or our small corner of it) again, that it may once again become beautiful and dramatic withal: for I do not believe they will have it dark and ugly for ever." This, one might think, was only that common impatience of the monotony of civilised life which turns some men into gamblers and makes others spend all their time in games and sport. But to Morris his own life was never monotonous. The dullness and ugliness that he saw were

75. *Autumn*, 1873.
   One of four panels of stained glass for the Inglenook fireplace, in the Dining Room of Cragside.
   Northumberland.

76. **Edward Burne-Jones** (for the design) and **Morris, Marshall, Faulkner & Co.** (for the production), *Elaine*, 1870.
   Stained and painted glass, 86.3 x 51.4 cm.
   Victoria & Albert Museum, London.

in the lives of others; and it was their failures that left him unsatisfied. We know from many things he said that the spectacle of our industrial society made him feel that there was something sinister in the order of the universe. The blind desire for life, which drives men to forego all that makes life worth living, seemed to him an evil thing which the men of the sagas had put away from them with all its attendant ignominy and fear. When he read the sagas he passed into a world where it did not exist, where it had never even been heard of. Whatever evil was done in them, and whatever sorrow was endured, was like the storm and grief of music that passes through all its changes to a glorious and intended close. But in the great mass of life as he saw it about him there seemed to be no intention either of God or of man. Men did what was not worth doing so that they might live; and lived so that they might do what was not worth doing. From this spectacle of futility he had turned away to his own happy work, to dreams out of which he made his art. But he had ceased to be content with dreams alone, and in the sagas had found as never before in any other stories a harmony and connection between dreams and reality. For in them nothing of reality is extenuated or set down in malice. Life is not made out to be better than it is, but it is faced so bravely and simply that it has all the glory of dreams. There is the same bravery, no doubt, in tragedies such as the *Agamemnon* and *King Lear*; but in them it is conscious. In the sagas it is unconscious both in the author and in all his characters. They never have to persuade themselves that life is worth living. That is implied in the very story; and, if they are subject to fate, it is rather a force within them, in which they exult, than a power that drives them before it. Reading the sagas Morris lost that youthful sense of the sharp division between the heart's desire and life's routine, which makes all purely romantic art and poetry. He began to feel that life itself might be like a saga to him, momentous even when it was sad; and he was drawn into it as the heroes of the sagas were drawn into battle.

One instance will show how completely the sagas possessed his imagination. At the end of his poem, *Iceland First Seen*, he rises into one of his moods of religious exaltation; and it is through a northern myth, though with a sudden personal rapture, that he expresses man's everlasting hope of a blessed state to be:

> "Ah! When thy Balder comes back And bears from the heart of the sun
> Peace and the healing of pain, And the wisdom that waiteth no more;
> And the lilies are laid on thy brow 'Mid the crown of the deeds thou hast done;
> And the roses spring up by thy feet That the rocks of the wilderness wore.
> Ah! When thy Balder comes back and we gather the gains he hath won,
> Shall we not linger a little to talk of thy sweetness of old,
> Yea turn back awhile to thy travail whence the Gods stood aloof to behold?"

This is addressed to Iceland, and we can understand from it why Iceland was to him what Greece is to some men. It was the country of mighty ghosts that drew him northward as other ghosts draw men southward.

77. **Dante Gabriel Rossetti** and **Edward Burne-Jones** (for the design) and **Morris, Marshall, Faulkner & Co.** (for the production),
Angel Swinging a Censer, 1870.
Stained glass window.
Bradford Art Galleries and Museum, West Yorkshire.

78. **Dante Gabriel Rossetti** and **Edward Burne-Jones** (for the design) and **Morris, Marshall, Faulkner & Co.** (for the production),
Seraphim, 1870.
Stained glass window.
Bradford Art Galleries and Museum, West Yorkshire.

79. **Dante Gabriel Rossetti** or **Edward Burne-Jones** (?) (for the design) and **Morris, Marshall, Faulkner & Co.** (for the production),
Three Angels, 1870.
Stained glass window removed from the East window of St James' Church, Brighouse, West Yorkshire (now demolished).
Bradford Art Galleries and Museums, West Yorkshire.

It was in 1871 that he first went there, and beforehand he took pleasure in practicing out-door cookery with children as a preparation for his long journeys in the wilderness. In his journals, published for the first time in the new collected edition of his works, we can read how he enjoyed the fun and adventure of these journeys; but the poems *Iceland First Seen* and *Gunnar's Howe* tell us why it seemed a second home to him. By nature he loved quiet, prosperous country best, with well-built farmhouses and cottages, and with all the signs of modest well-being. The mountainous wilderness of Iceland appalled him; but it was so glorified by the stories told about it that it seemed to him the counterpart of those stories in nature. He loved its poverty and bleakness because the spirit of man had taken on among them a fierce pure beauty like the beauty of mountain flowers. Indeed, he had the capacity, often found in men of genius, of admiring and absorbing qualities opposite to their own. His natural taste was for a dreamy richness and for things done, not slothfully, but with ease and luxuriance. If was his will, reacting against this natural taste, that made him love Iceland and all its stories and drove him at last into a struggle in which he did nothing easily and won no immediate success.

After Iceland he went to Italy for the first time in the spring of 1873; but he was already then hungering for another journey to the north; and Italy was too full of the works of the Renaissance and the Roman Empire to please him. "Do you suppose," he once said to a friend, "that I should see anything in Rome that I can't see in Whitechapel?" By that question he expressed his hatred for the Roman Empire and all its works; and his belief that its civilisation had taken a wrong turn like our own. To him the barbarians of the north were deliverers, and all their art, whether buildings or sagas, expressed the return of a right state of being, which might return for us also by means equally violent. After Italy he went to Iceland again with joy and relief, and this time travelled still further into the wilderness. "It was no idle whim that drew me there," he said, "but a true instinct for what I needed."

Morris translated the *Volsunga Saga* with Magnusson in 1870; and in the preface to their translation they speak of the nature and beauty with which the saga is filled. "We cannot doubt," they say, "that the reader will be intensely touched by finding, amidst all its wildness and remoteness, such startling realism, such subtlety, such close sympathy with all the passions that may move himself today." So Morris himself was drawn to it by its likeness, amid all unlikeness of circumstance, to reality as he saw it. And he thought it the finest story in the world, not because it was exciting or well constructed nor because it was romantically strange, but because in its very construction it seemed to him to express and reveal the great conflicting forces of life.

Thus *Sigurd the Volsung*, which was published in 1870, is a poem different in kind from most of the poems of *The Earthly Paradise*. He tells the story because of its likeness, not because of its unlikeness, to his own experience, and he creates it afresh in his own telling of it as if he were speaking of what he himself had seen and known.

He had done this to a lesser extent in *The Lovers of Gudrun*, but in that beautiful poem he used an old form of verse too light and too monotonous for his subject. For *Sigurd*

80. *Untitled*.
   Sketch for stained glass window.
   Private collection.

81. **John Henry Dearle** (for the design) and
   Morris & Co. (for the production), *Iris*, 1902.
   Wallpaper.
   Private collection.

he created a new metre which has all the momentum and variety that he needs. We have only to contrast the opening of the two poems to see the difference in their effect upon the ear and mind. *The Lovers of Gudrun* begins thus:

> Herdholt my tale names for the stead, where erst
> Olaf the Peacock dwelt, nowise the worst
> Among the great men of a noble day:
> Upon a knoll amid a vale it lay,
> Nigh where Laxriver meets the western sea,
> And in that day it nourished plenteously
> Grout wealth of sheep and cattle.

Here are the first, lines of *Sigurd*:

> There was a dwelling of Kings ere the world was waxen old;
> Dukes were the door-wards there, and the roofs were thatched with gold;
> Earls were the wrights that wrought it, and silver nailed its doors;
> Earl's wives were the weaving-women, queen's daughters strewed its floors.
> And the masters of its song-craft were the mightiest men that cast
> The sails of the storm of battle adown the bickering blast.

The first is a metre which only poetic matter can lift above prose; the second has power of its own to exalt the matter.

There is no English metre perfectly suited, like the Greek hexameter, to all the ups and downs of epic poetry. Blank verse has not enough momentum for narrative and can only be distinguished from prose in more prosaic passages by elaborate artifices of language, which impede the movement of the story. Rhymed ten-syllabled verse also lacks momentum and usually becomes rhetorical when it attempts grandeur, though it is well suited for romantic narrative, while storytelling in every kind of stanza is a kind of obstacle race, for there is an arbitrary check to the movement of the story at the end of each stanza. The metre of *Sigurd* is developed from the ancient and beautiful Saturnian metre: "The Queen was in her parlor eating bread and honey." Like that metre it has six stresses, but there is a less obvious break in the middle of the line; there are often more syllables to each stress; and the rhymes are single instead of double. All these changes are made to secure that continuity of sound so necessary to narrative poetry, and the metre in Morris's hands is capable of great variety. The type is a line such as this: "But Gunnar looked and considered and wise and wary he grew."

Here there is a break after *considered*, but it is not very marked because of the extra syllable before as well as after the central word. Sometimes the extra syllables are so evenly distributed that the break almost disappears: "Then he fondled its wail as it faded, and orderly over the strings." Here the line becomes simply a six-foot anapaest. But Morris employs this variation only in the more lyrical passages where he wishes to

82. *Wild Tulip*, 1884.
Pattern for wallpaper.
Dining Room, Wightwick Manor.

CHAP. XIII.

NOW weareth away the mid-winter, and when spring cometh, the weather groweth fair, the wood bloometh, the grass groweth, and ships may glide betwixt land and land.

So on a day the king says to his folk: "I will that ye come with us for our disport out into the woods, that we may look upon the fairness of the earth."

So did they, and went flock-meal with the king into the woods: but so it befell, that the king and Frithiof were gotten alone together afar from other men, and the king said he was heavy, and would fain sleep: then said Thief: "Get thee home, then, lord, for it better beseemeth men of high estate to lie at home than abroad."

"Nay," said the king, "so will I not do." And he laid him down therewith, and slept fast, snoring loud. Thief sat close by him, and presently drew his sword from his sheath, & cast it far away from him.

A little while after the king woke up, and said: "Was it not so, Frithiof, that a many things came into thy mind een now? but well hast thou dealt with them, and great honour shalt thou have of me. Lo now, I knew thee straightway, that first evening thou camest into our hall: now nowise speedily shalt thou depart from us; and somewhat great abideth thee."

Said Frithiof: "Lord king, thou hast done to me well, and in friendly wise; but yet must I get me gone soon, because my company cometh speedily to meet me, as I have given them charge to do."

So then they rode home from the wood, and the king's folk came flocking to him, and home they fared to the hall and drank joyously: and it was made known to all folk that Frithiof the Bold had been abiding there through the winter-tide.

CHAP. XIV.

EARLY of a morning-tide one smote on the door of that hall, wherein slept the king and queen, and many others: then the king asked who it was that called at the hall door; and so he who was without said: "Here am I, Frithiof; and I am arrayed for my departure."

Then was the door opened, and Frithiof came in, and sang a stave:

Have great thanks for the guesting
Thou gavest with all bounty;
Dight fully for departure
Is the eagles' feeder now;
But Ingibiorg I mind thee
While yet on earth I dwell;
Live gloriously! I give thee
This gift for many kisses.

39   40

give the effect of an irresistible impetus overcoming all obstacles. This effect he could not obtain if the reader's ear did not expect a break in the middle of the line.

The defect of the metre is that it seems to express more excitement than can be sustained in a long narrative poem. It is not suited, like the Greek hexameter, to passages of noble calm or to matter-of-fact statement. But it has a wider range than any other English metre that has been applied to epic; and Morris was able to invent it and use it epically, because his mind stayed at an epic height all through the poem. *Sigurd* falls far short of *Paradise Lost* in lofty contemplation, and there are no isolated passages in it to compare with the finest in that poem. But we read *Sigurd*, as we do not read *Paradise Lost*, for the story, which is perhaps the grandest ever conceived by the mind of man, and we never feel the treatment to be unequal to the theme. Indeed, Morris tells the tale as if from his own experience, not as if he had plucked it from the past merely as a pretext for writing poetry; he was able to do so because his own conception of life – like the conception of the saga – was heroic. Indeed, the prophesy made over the new-born Sigurd might have been made of Morris himself could any one have foreseen his future when he was a child:

> But there rose up a man most ancient, and he cried: 'Hail, Dawn of the Day!
> How many things shalt thou quicken, how many shall, thou slay!
> How many things shalt thou waken, how many lull to sleep!
> How many shalt thou scatter, how many gather and keep!
> O me, how thy love shall cherish, how thine hate shall wither and burn!
> How the hope shall be sped from thy right hand, nor the fear to thy left return!
> O thy deeds that men shall sing of! O thy deeds that the gods shall see!
> O Sigurd, son of the Volsungs, O Victory yet to be!'

In the saga itself we are told simply that "Hjordis brought forth a man-child, who was straightly borne before King Hjalprek, and then was the King glad thereof, when he saw the keen eyes in the head of him, and he said that few men would be equal to him or like unto him in any wise." This is only one instance out of many of the manner in which Morris drew poetry out of the story rather than embroidered it with versified ornament. He never adds to it anything incongruous with its nature, yet he never puts an archaic restraint upon himself. He moves as freely in it as Tolstoy in *War and Peace*; and the battles of which he tells do not seem to be old, unhappy, far-off things, but to result from the same conflict of forces that produces the strife of our own time. Yet there is no allegory in *Sigurd*. The characters have their own life; and Regin the smith only speaks like Morris himself because in all ages the artist has the same joys and labours:

> And to me, the least and the youngest, what gift for the slaying of case?
> Save the grief that remembers the past, and the fear that the future sees;
> And the hammer and fashioning-iron, and the living coal of fire;
> And the craft that createth a semblance, and fails of the heart's desire;
> And the toil that each dawning quickens and the task that is never done;
> And the heart that longeth ever, nor will look to the deed that is won.

83. **William Morris, Charles Fairfax Murray, Louise Powell** and **Graily Herwitt**, *The Story of Frithiof the Bold*, c. 1873. Watercolour and gilding on paper, 40.1 x 53 cm (open book). Paul Getty Library, Wormsley.

It is easy to see and name the faults of *Sigurd*. Morris wrote it, as he wrote nearly everything, too quickly. There are rough lines in it and vague passages. There are catch-words and phrases, and sometimes the style and metre both seem mechanical. We cannot but wish that he had spent ten years on it instead of one, labouring at those passages in which his inspiration failed him, for it is by such labour that an artist learns to correct his faults and acquires unexpected powers.

But *Sigurd*, with all its faults, is an epic poem to be read for its story. Its excellence is in the whole, not in detachable parts, in design, not in ornament. It has a cumulative power possessed by no other modern narrative poem in English. It was grandly conceived before it was written; and its defects of detail do not obscure the conception. Nothing but the modern passion for realistic illusion could have made the public blind to the reality of *Sigurd*. That passion makes the reader's interest dependent on circumstance, and *Sigurd* is about people and things unlike those we read about in the newspaper. It is not even a romantic poem interesting for the strangeness of its circumstance. To Morris himself the story is not outlandish. He said that it ought to be to the peoples of the north what the *Tale of Troy* was to the Greeks. We may say that it was to him what the finest of our Bible stories are to most of us. He was so familiar with it, it had sunk into his mind so thoroughly, that he no more thought of treating it romantically or of heightening its interest with local colour than Fra Angelico thought of introducing local colour into his sacred paintings. And as Fra Angelico painted for a public familiar with his subjects, so Morris wrote as if the public were equally familiar with his story. This, probably, is the reason why it has never been read or admired as much as it deserves. But unless our world loses its love of poetry altogether it will meet with its deserts at last.

Morris as a Socialist

Morris was first drawn into public life almost against his will and not by any sudden conviction that he ought to take part in it. Up to the year 1877, when he was forty-four, he had concerned himself with politics, and, indeed, with any kind of public action, less than most men of his class. He lacked the superior person's contempt of political parties, but they and their behaviour and the excitement which they aroused, puzzled him as men who do not hunt or shoot are puzzled by the ardour of those who do. He had no natural liking for public meetings or political discussions; indeed, he had a natural dislike for them, and he needed to be powerfully moved by some particular event before he could be induced to take part in any kind of public action. One of the first events that so moved him was not political at all. But the action which it provoked was important, not only for its immediate results, but because it introduced him into public life and made him aware that he could do some good by means of appeals to the public.

In 1876 he was moved to indignation by the restoration of Lichfield Cathedral and of the parish church at Burford, a beautiful village near his own Kelmscott. Then, in the spring of 1877, hearing that Tewkesbury Abbey was also threatened with restoration,

84. **Walter Crane**,
Hammersmith Branch Socialist League
(Membership card for Henry Halliday Sparling),
1890.
Ink on paper, 11.4 x 7.6 cm.
Signed by Emery Walker and William Morris.
Private collection.

SOCIALIST LEAGUE

HAMMERSMITH BRANCH

BRANCH SECRETARY. Emery Walker

TREASURER. William Morris

he wrote a letter to the *Athenæum* proposing that "an association should be set on foot to keep a watch on old monuments, to protest against all 'restoration' that means more than keeping out wind and weather, and, by all means, literary and others, to awaken a feeling that our ancient buildings are not mere ecclesiastical toys, but sacred monuments of the nation's growth and hope."

About a month after this letter was published, the *Society for the Protection of Ancient Buildings* was founded. Morris himself became secretary of it, and wrote a statement of the principles which it was founded to uphold. It was for the protection, he said, of any building "that could be looked upon as artistic, picturesque, historical, antique or substantial: any work, in short, over which educated artistic people would think it worth while to argue at all." Its principle was "to put Protection in the place of Restoration, to stave off decay by daily care, to prop a perilous wall or mend a leaking roof by such means as were obviously meant for support or covering, and showed no pretence of other art; and otherwise to resist all tampering with either the fabric or ornament of the building as it stands."

Morris gave much time and trouble to the business of the society for the rest of his life, though after a time Thackeray Turner became secretary. To the devoted labours of those two men we chiefly owe it that many of our beautiful old buildings have not been turned into dull new ones. They became the terror of evil-designing architects all over the country; and, more important even than that, by pointing out the absurdity of copying old buildings, they made architects and the public alike understand better how to obtain the qualities they desired in new buildings.

It was in 1876 that Morris first took any part in politics; and then he was concerned with the action of our statesmen, not at home, but abroad. In that year a society called the Eastern Question Association was founded to protest against the indifference of the Conservative Government to the Bulgarian Atrocities. Russia, whatever her motive, wished to prevent the Turks from continuing those atrocities, and the British Government was supporting Turkey against Russia. Morris became treasurer of the Association, and in a letter to his friend Faulkner he gave his reasons for doing so:

"As to the Russians, all I say is this: we might have noted so that they could have had no pretext for interfering with Turkey except in accordance with the unanimous wish of Europe: we have so acted as to drive them into separate interference whatever may come: and to go to war with them for this would be a piece of outrageous injustice. Furthermore, if we came victorious out of such a war, what should we do with Turkey, if we did not wish to be damned? 'Take it ourselves,' says the bold man, 'and rule it as we rule India.' But the bold man doesn't live in England at present, I think; and I know what the Tory trading, stock-jobbing scoundrel that one calls an Englishman today would do with it; he would shut his eyes hard over it, get his widows and orphans to lend it money, and sell it vast quantities of bad cotton."

85. *Columbine*, 1876.
Design for chintz.
Pencil, pen, ink and watercolour.
Victoria & Albert Museum, London.

This letter shows that Morris already despised and distrusted the English governing classes. He openly showed his contempt and distrust of them in a manifesto, which he addressed to the workingmen of England in May 1877 after Russia had declared war on Turkey.

"Who are they who are leading us into war?" he asked. "Greedy gamblers on the Stock Exchange, idle officers of the army and navy (poor fellows!), worn-out mockers of the clubs, desperate purveyors of exciting war-news for the comfortable breakfast tables of those who have nothing to lose by war; and lastly, in the place of honour, the Tory Rump, that we fools, weary of peace, reason and justice, chose at the last election to represent us." He goes on to tell them that they do not know "the bitterness of hatred against freedom and progress that lies at the hearts of a certain part of the richer classes in this country." Those men, he says, "If they had the power (may England perish rather!) would thwart your just aspirations, would silence you, would deliver you bound hand and foot for ever to irresponsible capital."

Thus, while to most Liberals the Eastern Question was one of foreign politics to be settled by the ordinary political means, to Morris it was only the symptom of a much larger social question. He saw the policy of the government as the sin of the governing classes, and he appealed for them to the governed. The Association was, in the main, a society of Liberals, many of whom wished to use it as a party instrument. Thus, as war became more and more popular with the mob, the Association's opposition to it weakened. At last, in February 1878, it refused to hold a meeting at which Gladstone had consented to speak. This was one of the first of those ominous examples of the cowardice of a minority in the face of a noisy majority, of which we have since seen so many in England; and it disgusted Morris with party politics altogether. "I am out of it now," he said, "I mean as to bothering my head about it. I shall give up reading the papers and shall stick to my work."

But he was not out of it for good, as he was soon to discover, and meanwhile this short experience of politics had the important result that it gave him some experience of the radical workingman. When war with Russia was threatened at the beginning of 1878, he wrote that he was astonished at the folly that could play with such tremendous tools, and he meant the folly of the governing classes. "More and more I feel," he says, "how entirely right the flattest democracy is." Morris, though born a member of the middle classes, had long ceased to be one of them; he possessed none of their hopes or fears, their sense of propriety or their scale of values. He was himself a workman and naturally more at ease with workmen than with professors. To his own workmen he was masterful enough at times, but as their foreman not as their social superior. He lost his temper with them sometimes, but always as man with man, and they recognised one of their own when he did so. It was through being a workman himself that he became aware of the evils which prevented men from doing good work or taking pleasure in it; and it was not mere sentimentality which led him to believe that other workmen must also be more aware of those evils and more anxious to end them than the upper and middle classes.

86. *The Story of the Glittering Plain*, 1894.
Design for the title-page,
graphite and ink, 35.6 x 25.4 cm.

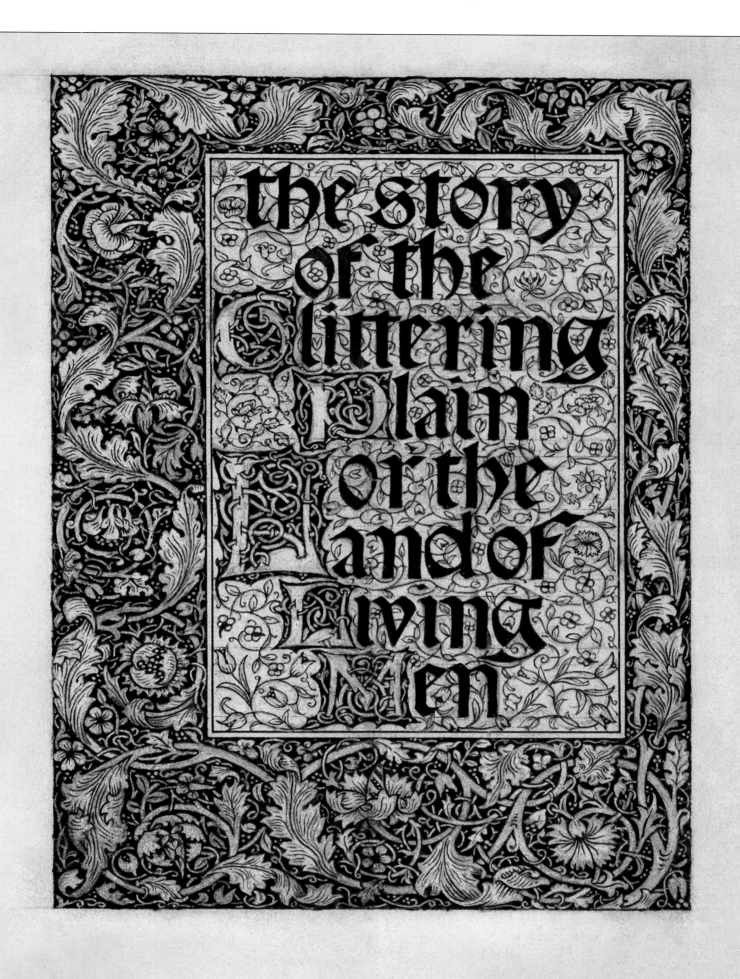

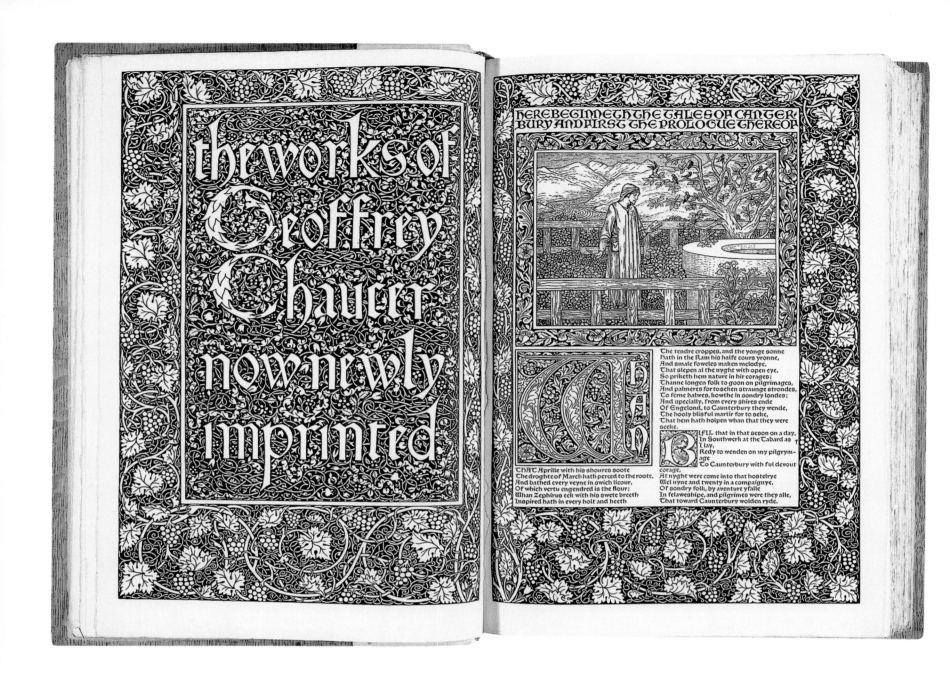

87. *The Works of Geoffrey Chaucer*, 1896.

Kelmscott Press Book.

Paper, 42.5 x 29.2 cm (leaf).

Art Gallery and Museum, Cheltenham.

Yet he still called himself a Liberal and was treasurer of the National Liberal League, a body composed mainly of radical workingmen, until 1881. But when the Liberals came into power and proceeded to pass the Irish Coercion Bill it seemed to him that their name was only a label. The National Liberal League ceased to exist, and Morris said that everything was as vague in politics as in art. It was this vagueness that troubled him even more than the evils that so plainly needed a remedy. He wrote in 1880:

"I am in rather a discouraged mood, and the whole thing seems almost, too tangled to see through and too heavy to move. Happily though, I am not bound either to see through it or move it but a very little way: meanwhile I do know what I love and what I hate, and believe that neither the love nor the hatred are matters of accident or of whim."

This certainty of his own loves and hatreds was the foundation of all his future beliefs, and it was a surer foundation than many practical statesmen, who do not know what they themselves want in life, ever find for their politics. Thus, a year later he writes with less bewilderment: "My mind is very full of the great change which I hope is slowly coming over the world, and of which surely this new year will be one of the landmarks." And six months later he says that thinking people are being driven from all interest in politics save in revolutionary politics: "which I must say seems like to be my case." "All political change," he writes, "seems to me useful now as making it possible to get the social one."

All through the years 1881 and 1882 he reflected on social questions, and now and again expressed something of what he thought in a letter. "I feel a lonely kind of chap," he said, as if aware that none of his friends could help him in this growing trouble of his mind. Indeed, no two of his friends, Mr. Mackail tells us, are agreed in their view of the steps by which he became a Socialist. In those two years he seems to have experienced that kind of conversion which has driven some men into monasteries and has sent others to preach to the heathen. He must have seen his future beliefs before him and must have known that, if they became his, they would distract him from the work that he loved. For he was one of those men to whom belief always means action and who cannot hold opinions as intellectual luxuries. It is quite easy to hold revolutionary opinions if they make no difference to your conduct. But Morris had kept out of politics for many years because he knew that, if he went into them, they would make a difference to his conduct. Indeed, he was like those men who avoid religion because they are afraid of what it would do with them. And just as they feel that it is always lying in wait for them until at last they give all their souls up to it, so his mind was beset by thoughts about the state of the world that at last he could no longer withstand. Of his own work he wrote in 1882: "It does sometimes seem to me a strange thing that a man should be driven to work with energy and even with pleasure and enthusiasm at work which he knows will serve no end but amusing himself. Am I doing nothing but make-believe, then, like Louis XVI's lock-making?" He had the same feeling about other men's art. He could not read Swinburne's *Tristram of Lyonesse*, he said. *"Nothing could lay hold of me at all."* And he goes on, thinking no doubt of himself just as much as of Swinburne, and speaking as if he were Tolstoy:

> "In these days when all the arts, even poetry, are like to be overwhelmed under the mass of material riches which civilisation has made and is making more and more hastily every day; riches which the world has made indeed, but cannot use to any good purpose: in these days the issue between art, that is, the godlike part of man, and mere bestiality, is so momentous, and the surroundings of life are so stern and unplayful, that nothing can take serious hold of people, or should do so, but that which is rooted deepest in reality and is quite at first hand; there is no room for anything which is not forced out of a man of deep feeling because of its innate strength and vision."

Henceforward, indeed, nearly all his own art and poetry was to seem a kind of stolen pleasure to him, and he could hardly have produced it at all if he had not been able to do in his leisure as much as other great artists can do in their working hours. For years there had been growing upon him the sense that something momentous was happening in the minds of men. That change which was slowly working in his own mind seemed to him a turning point in the history of our civilisation, and indeed, it was a symptom of great moment. "The consciousness of revolution stirring," he said, "prevented me, luckier than many others of artistic perceptions, from crystallising into a mere railer against progress on the one hand, and on the other from wasting time and energy in any of the numerous schemes by which the quasi-artistic of the middle classes hope to make art grow when it has no longer any root." The revolution was mainly in his own mind at that time, and had not yet happened as he expected it, any more than the millennium happened as the early Christians expected it. But they worked a vast change upon the world of which their expectation was itself a symptom; and so Morris's expectation was the symptom of a change that is even now only beginning to work upon us. He saw that society, as it was constituted, could not provide the kind of life that he wished to live, except for a few fortunate individuals; and that even they could not stay untroubled in their earthly Paradise except by shutting their eyes to everything outside it. With him the immense complacency of the Victorians came to an end. There had, of course, always been discontent among the poor, but Morris, with all his prosperity, came to feel that discontent as if he were one of them. He no longer believed that they were merely the inevitable waste of the best system that could be devised, any more than they believed it. He judged the system by its effects upon them, and with a fiercer condemnation because he knew, by his own experience, the difference between their lives and life as it might be. And it was this power in him, of seeing things as if he were himself one of those whom he pitied, that made him a revolutionary Socialist.

Morris felt the difference between an advanced Radical and a revolutionary Socialist to be sharp and clear. Radicalism ceased to satisfy him because, he thought, it was mainly concerned with political machinery. Its implied axiom, as it seemed to him, was that, if political machinery is put right, economic conditions will also right themselves, so far as they can be righted by the will of man. He had taken little interest hitherto in political machinery because, in the hands of Liberals and Conservatives alike, it seemed to him to produce no effects of any value. For a time, therefore, he believed that nothing could be done with it and that a man like himself must leave the parties to play their own game. When he became a Socialist, he believed that political machinery should be directly employed to improve economic conditions, and that, if it were so used, would improve them. Political freedom and equality might satisfy the Radical, but Morris held that they were only a means to the end of economic equality, and that without it they were valueless. The Radical believes that all the reform which he desires can be carried by purely constitutional means; and in England at any rate, there is little fear nowadays that any purely political change, demanded by a majority of the electors, will promote civil war. Morris, when he became a Socialist, wished for economic changes, which he expected, would provoke a civil war. The rich, he thought, would submit to political changes because they knew that no purely political change would destroy their economic power, and because they knew also that economic power always means political power, whatever form a constitution may take. He wished to destroy their economic power; and, if necessary, he was prepared to do that by means of revolution and civil war.

88. *Circular*, c. 1897.

    Showing examples of the Golden,
    Troy and Chaucer typefaces, 20.3 x 14.6 cm.

KELMSCOTT PRESS, UPPER
MALL, HAMMERSMITH.

July 28th, 1897.

Note. This is the Golden type.
This is the Troy type.
This is the Chaucer type.

Secretary:
S. C. Cockerell, Kelmscott Press, Upper Mall,
Hammersmith, London, W., to whom all
letters should be addressed. *or to*

Morris & Company
449 Oxford Street
London W.

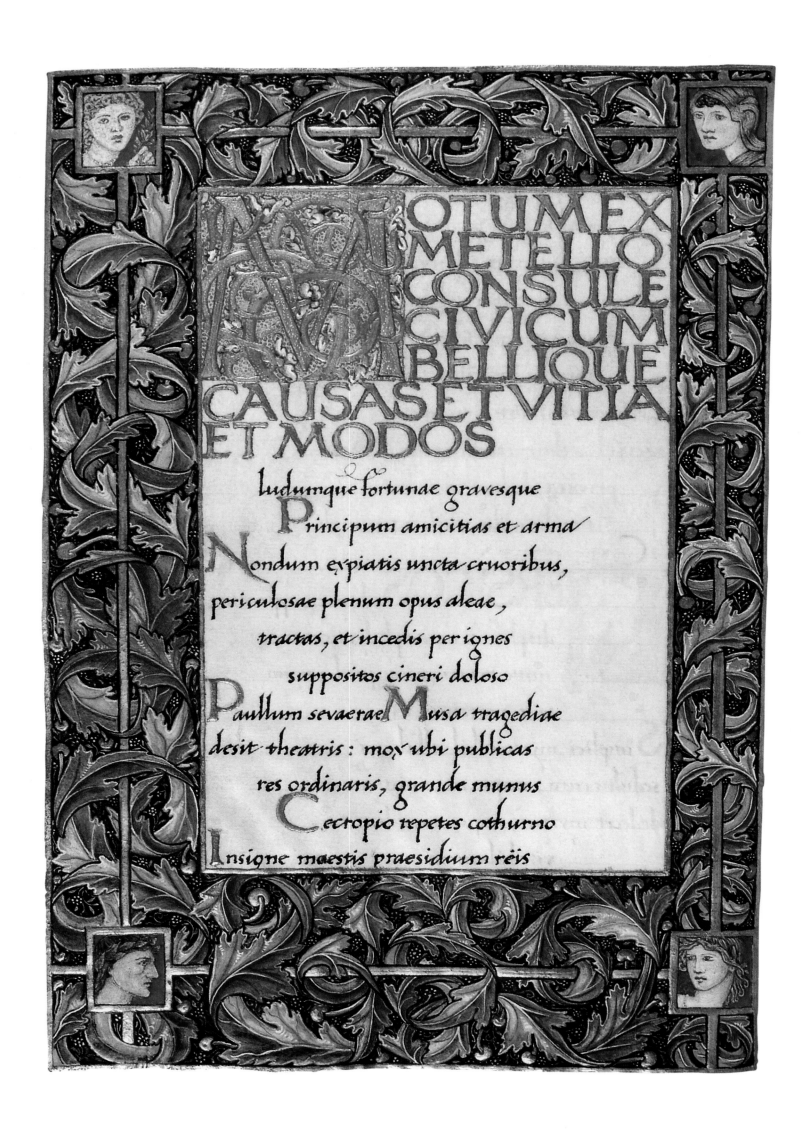

NOTUM EX METELLO CONSULE CIVICUM BELLIQUE CAUSAS ET VITIA ET MODOS

ludumque fortunae gravesque
Principum amicitias et arma
Nondum expiatis uncta cruoribus,
periculosae plenum opus aleae,
tractas, et incedis per ignes
suppositos cineri doloso
Paullum sevaerae Musa tragediae
desit theatris: mox ubi publicas
res ordinaris, grande munus
Cecropio repetes cothurno
Insigne maestis praesidium reis

About this part of his creed there is no doubt whatever. Indeed, it was his hope that a new and better society might be made by revolution that turned him into a Socialist. If he had not had that hope he could never have taken any interest in politics after he lost all faith in the Liberal party. He saw society as a class war already existing, but only conscious on the part of the rich and concealed by them under the unrealities of the party conflict. His aim was to make the poor conscious of this war, to show them what evils they had to fight against, and to convince them that by fighting they could end them. He never made any concealment of this aim, and we cannot doubt that, if the revolution which he hoped for had come in his time, he would have been a revolutionary leader; or that, if it had failed, he would have been put to death by the victors. He might also, if it had degenerated into a terror, have been put to death by the victors of his own side. But even then, we may be sure, he would have died with courage and without despair.

It was on the 17th of January 1883, that he declared himself a Socialist by becoming a member of the *Democratic Federation*; and in doing so he enlisted as a private who was ready to obey orders. *"I put some conscience,"* he said, *"into trying to learn the economical side of Socialism, and even tackled Marx, though I suffered agonies of confusion of the brain over reading the economics of that work."* People have supposed from confessions of this kind that Morris was slightly confused about things. Many sayings of his own, and, indeed, the mass of his writings about art, prove that he was most clear-headed about any subject in which he took an interest. But he took little interest in economics; and, as Mackail says, his Socialism "was not the outcome of

89. *Odes of Horace*, 1874.
   Illustrated page of the manuscript.
   Bodleian Library, University of Oxford.

90. *Kennet*, 1883.
   Furnishing fabric. Jacquard-woven silk and linen,
   69.8 x 70.4 cm.
   Victoria & Albert Museum, London.

abstract economic reasoning." It was the outcome of a belief that men can, by collective action, obtain what they desire, if they know clearly what it is and if it is in itself desirable. He himself knew very clearly what kind of life he desired and he knew that his task as a Socialist was to communicate that desire and to make it clear to others. In political movements, as in everything else, there must be division of labour, as the labourers themselves have different powers. The theorist may not be a good organiser or the organiser an eloquent speaker. Morris had been learning all his life what is best worth having in life; and he had come to the conclusion that it was incompatible with the present state of society. He had not been learning to speak or to organise or to prove economic propositions. He brought his own contribution to Socialism and it was a contribution of the greatest value; for he made Socialism seem to thousands a thing desirable in itself, because he showed them the kind of civilisation it should aim at.

Meanwhile he was ready to do what his leaders told him to do, although from the first he was too wise to expect any perfection of wisdom in them. A few months after he had joined the *Democratic Federation* he became a member of its executive. "I don't like belonging to a body without knowing what they are doing," he wrote. "Without feeling very sanguine about their doings, they seem certainly to mean something. Money is chiefly lacking, as usual." He himself supplied as much of the money as he could, selling most of his valuable books for the purpose. He began to write Socialist songs, to lecture on Socialism, and, what he disliked most, to speak at street corners. "I am sure it is right," he wrote in a letter, "whatever the apparent consequences may be, to stir up the lower classes (damn the word) to demand a higher standard of life for themselves, not merely for themselves or for the sake of the national comfort it will bring, but for the good of the whole world and the regeneration of the conscience of man." So he set to work to stir them up by the most direct means as he had set to work to learn arts when he wished to revive them. "Our business is to make Socialists," he said; and through all disappointments and bewilderments he continued to say this and to act upon it.

The *Democratic Federation* changed its name to the *Social* so that there should be no doubt about its Socialism. On January 4, 1884, appeared the first issue of its weekly paper *Justice*, to which Morris contributed both money and writing; but the Federation had already begun to suffer from those discords that are common to all revolutionary bodies without political power. Practical politics may be demoralising, but they train men to act together. They impose a kind of military discipline which may lead to sacrifice of principle, but which also suppresses egotism. The Federation lacked this discipline; it was an association of revolutionaries, many of whom had nothing in common except that they wanted a revolution, and who soon began to quarrel among themselves. Hyndman, the leader of one party in the Federation, was, and still is, a Marxist, and to him the whole body of Marx's doctrine is the Socialist orthodoxy. He maintained it with admirable persistency all his life; and his aim was to make and keep the Federation a Marxist body. He wished it to be as unanimous as a Cabinet always pretends to be; but to Morris, since it was not a cabinet, this unanimity seemed unnecessary. He wished it to be a propagandist rather than a political body, and he was ready to work with any one

91. *The Aeneids of Virgil*, 1874-1875.
Illustrated page of the manuscript.

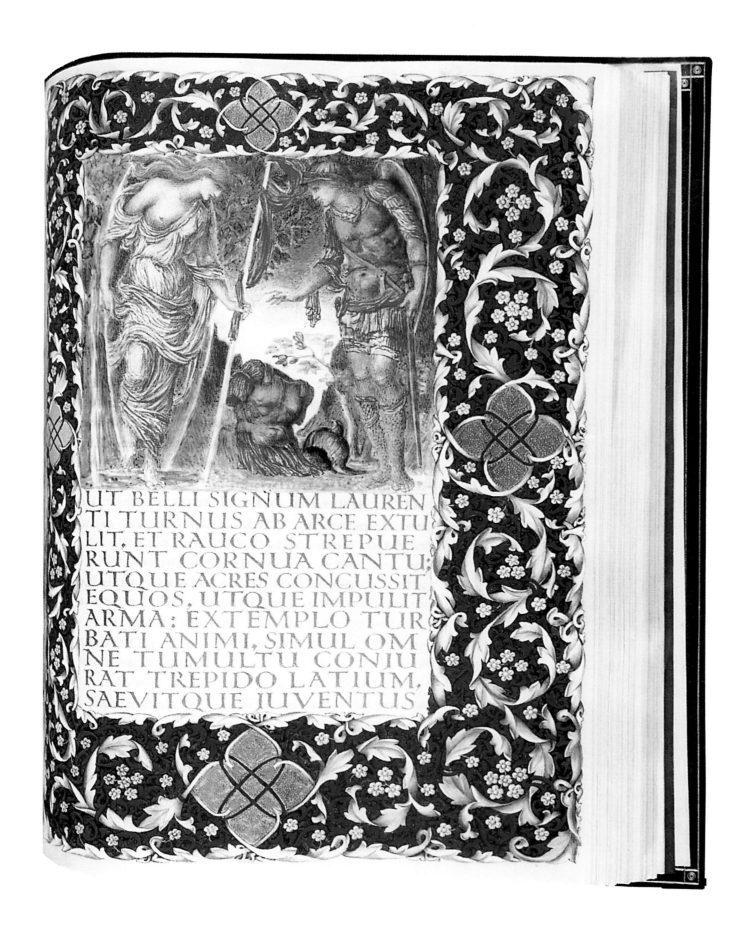

UT BELLI SIGNUM LAUREN
TI TURNUS AB ARCE EXTU
LIT, ET RAUCO STREPUE
RUNT CORNUA CANTU,
UTQUE ACRES CONCUSSIT
EQUOS, UTQUE IMPULIT
ARMA: EXTEMPLO TUR
BATI ANIMI, SIMUL OM
NE TUMULTU CONIU
RAT TREPIDO LATIUM,
SAEVITQUE IUVENTUS

The blue panelling comes up to this line.

who in the main desired what he desired. Thus he was impatient of the strict orthodoxy of Mr. Hyndman and, because of his reputation, was forced unwillingly to become Hyndman's chief opponent in the Federation. He wrote in August 1884:

"Practically, it comes to a contest between him and me. If I don't come up to the scratch I shall disappoint those who, I believe, have their hearts in the cause and are quite disinterested, many of them simple and worthy people. I don't think intrigue and ambition are amongst my many faults; but here I am driven to thrust myself forward and making a party within a party."

Hyndman was by nature a practical politician. Morris was not, and from first to last he believed that the time had not yet come for Socialists to take part in practical politics. "Our business," he said, "is the making of Socialists, i.e., convincing people that Socialism is good for them and is possible. When we have brought people to that way of thinking, they will find out what action is necessary for putting their principles in practice. Therefore, I say, make Socialists. We Socialists can do nothing else that is useful." Sometimes he hoped for a social revolution soon; sometimes he saw that it was far off, but he always said that there were not yet enough Socialists to make a powerful political party, and therefore he did not wish them to imitate the organisation of a political party or to aim at its practical unanimity. He also believed that, so long as Socialists were few, they would only dilute their principles if they tried to enforce them in practical politics. There were not yet enough of them to leaven the whole mass, and if any of them succeeded in getting into Parliament they would find themselves subdued in that body. Whatever society he belonged to he wished to be a propagandist rather than political, and the real cause of his difference with Hyndman was that the latter wished the Federation to be political as well as propagandist.

But the quarrel came to a head on a point of detail now of no interest. There was a meeting in December 1884, which lasted four and a half hours, at the end of which Morris and his party, in a majority, resigned to form another body, which they called the Socialist League. Morris had no open quarrel with the remaining members of the Federation, and afterwards occasionally wrote for Justice. Hyndman, who makes no pretence of loving his enemies, acknowledged Morris's generosity and praised him with equal generosity.

"This morning," Morris wrote on the 28th of December, "I hired very humble quarters for the Socialist League... So there I am, really once more like a young bear with all my troubles before me." There he spoke even more truly, perhaps, than he knew, for he was to have as much trouble with the new League as with the old Federation. There were the same causes of discord in it, the same struggles between opportunists and extremists, and in this case the extremists won and at last drove Morris out of the League after he had endured much at their hands.

The organ of the League was called the "Commonweal", and its first issue appeared in February 1885. Morris was editor and also treasurer of the League, himself supplying

92. **Philip Webb**, *Design for the wall-decoration and cornice in the Green Dining Room*, 1866. Pencil, watercolour, body colour and gold, 47.6 x 29.7 cm. Victoria & Albert Museum, London.

93. *The Roots of the Mountains*, 1890.
Book bounded in block-printed linen
Honeysuckle, 19.5 x 16 cm (leaf).
Victoria & Albert Museum, London.

most of the money that he treasured. Much of the prose that he wrote for it is no better, either in spirit or in execution, than the stuff ordinarily produced by political hacks for a living, but in the March issue appeared the *Message of the March Wind*, the first part of a narrative poem, *The Pilgrims of Hope*, which was published by instalment in the paper, and which contains, perhaps, the finest passages of poetry that he ever wrote.

From this time and for some years he worked desperately hard, preaching Socialism and writing about it. Yet he was under no illusions about the present importance of his League or the stir it was likely to make in the world. He spoke of "the petty skirmish of outposts, the light of a corporal's guard in which I am immediately concerned," but, he adds, "I have more faith than a grain of mustard seed in the future history of 'civilisation,' which I know now is doomed to destruction, and probably before very long... I used really to despair once because I thought what the idiots of our day used to call progress would go on perfecting itself: happily I know now that all that will have a sudden check – sudden in appearance I mean – 'as it was in the days of Noe.' "Here he talks like Carlyle; and, indeed, he was enjoying all the delight of a fierce reaction against those notions of a mechanical progress by means of which so many good men of his time managed to content themselves with society as it was. That progress had been a nightmare of optimism to him, and he had woken out of it into the daylight of his own eager pessimism, in which at least he could exercise his will, as a man fighting with other men. He writes in May 1885:

"On Sunday, I went a-preaching Stepney way... You would perhaps have smiled at my congregation: some twenty people in a little room as dirty as convenient and stinking a good deal. It took the fire out of my fine periods, I can tell you; it is a great drawback that I can't talk to them roughly and unaffectedly. Also, I would like to know what amount of real feeling underlies their bombastic revolutionary talk when they get to that. I don't seem to have got at them yet. You see this great class gulf lies between us."

Morris did not like speaking and had little natural gift for it. That is why he found it so difficult to talk to his audiences, for only a born speaker can do that. He learnt in time to say what he wanted to say, but speaking never became one of the many arts that he practiced for the love of them. He always breakfasted with the Burne-Jones family on Sunday, and often Lady Burne-Jones tells us, he would leave in the middle of the morning for his street preaching.

"The simplicity with which he did this was fine to see. Consider what it must have meant for him to leave, and to speak, as he frequently did, either at a street corner near his own house – where he was but a prophet in his own country – or perhaps miles away at Ball's Pond, where he was not of as much importance in the neighbourhood as a cheap-jack."

Every man who does certain things very well and has won fame by doing them, has a natural dislike of attempting other things, which he does indifferently, among people who are indifferent to him. But Morris was as free from vanity as any man can be, and he did not even pity himself. "I am not over-inclined for my morning preachment at Walham Green," he wrote, "but go I must, as also to Victoria Park in the afternoon. I had a sort of dastardly hope that it might rain. Mind you, I don't pretend to say I don't like it in some way or other; like it when I am on my legs, if I flow."

But it was not his proper business and he forced himself to do it, well knowing that. Indeed, fiercely as he talked and felt, he did not wish to be fierce, and was angry with things because they stirred an unwelcome anger in him. He wrote:

"I do not love contention, I even shrink from it with indifferent persons. Indeed, I know that all my faults lie on the other side: love of ease, dreaminess, sloth, sloppy good nature, are what I chiefly accuse myself of. All those could not have been hurt by my being a 'moderate Socialist'; nor need I have forfeited a good share of the satisfaction of vainglory, for in such a party I could easily have been a leader, nay, perhaps the leader, whereas amidst our rough work I can scarcely be a leader at all, and certainly do not care to be."

But he was not merely mortifying himself in the hope that he might find peace and salvation for his troubled soul. He believed that he could do no good by patronising the Socialist movement as if he were a royal personage opening a charity bazaar.

Whatever the waste of his own powers, he was determined to fight for it, as French artists and poets fought for their country in the siege of Paris. And he never pitied himself for this waste; indeed, he felt rather that he could not do or give enough. There is a passage in the *Pilgrims of Hope* where he speaks his own thoughts through the mouth of the hero, contrasting the lot of the rich and the poor rebel:

When the poor man thinks – and rebels, the whip lies ready a near;
But he who is rebel and rich may live safe for many a year,
While he warms his heart with pictures of all the glory to come.
There's the storm of the press and the critics maybe, but sweet is his home.
There is meat in the noon and the even and rest when the day is done,
All is fair and orderly there as the rising and setting sun.

So he was very patient of the quarrels and absurdities of the League. It was a body, Miss May Morris tells us:

"[A body] made up of the most varied elements, and the wonder is, not so much that divergences became evident once more as time went on, but that we ever held together at all: there were members of the Radical working men's clubs, members of the old International, old men who remembered the times written of in the 'Communist Manifesto' of 1847... there was the drift from early Socialist bodies Owenites. Chartists, Co-operators; there were some professional and literary men and the Universities were represented... There was a foreign spy or two and a sprinkling of wastrels who made one's heart ache for their uselessness and the knowledge that none of their life was in their own hands to make or mar."

Morris himself had no illusions about the League, yet he made the best of it:

"Even such things as this, the army setting off to conquer all the world, turning back to burn Jack's pig-sty, and tumbling drunk into the fire. Even this doesn't shake me; means we must use the best we can get; but one thing I won't do, wait forever till perfect means are made for very imperfect me to work with."

Having the gift of expression he was able to ease his disgust with a phrase; having the power of thought he was able to establish and define his own attitude to all those troublesome people; but they themselves could do none of those things, and therefore he pitied them and bore with them as being less fortunate than himself. The main quarrel, he tells us, was again between the two sections, parliamentary and anti-parliamentary, "which are pretty much commensurate with the Collectivists and Anarchists." He tried to compose this quarrel because, he said, "there are a good many who would join the Anarchist side who are not really Anarchists, and who would be useful to us; indeed, I doubt, if except one or two Germans, etc., we have any real Anarchists amongst us, and I don't want to see a lot of enthusiastic men who are not very deep in Socialist doctrines driven off for a fad of

94. Detail from "*Love Fulfilled*", a poem from *A Book of Verse* (1870), written and illuminated as a gift for Georgiana Burne-Jones.

95. Ceiling Paper.
    Designed for St James' Palace.

96. Tapestry.

HAST thou longed through weary days
For the sight of one loved face,
Hast thou cried aloud for rest,
Mid the pain of sundering hours,
Cried aloud for sleep and death
Since the sweet unhoped for best
Was a shadow and a breath —
O, long now, for no fear lowers
O'er these faint feet-kissing flowers
O, rest now; and yet in sleep
All thy longing shalt thou keep.

Thou shalt rest, and have no fear
Of a dull awaking near,
Of a life for ever blind,
Uncontent and waste and wide.
Thou shalt wake, and think it sweet
That thy love is near and kind.
Sweeter still for lips to meet;
Sweetest, that thine heart doth hide
Longing all unsatisfied
With all longing's answering
Howsoever close ye cling

153

the more pedantic part of the Collectivist section." He himself could side with neither party, for he was neither an Anarchist nor a parliamentarian. Some day, he said, it might be necessary for Socialists to go into Parliament, "but that could only be when we are very much more advanced than we are now; in short, on the verge of a revolution, so that we might either capture the army or shake their confidence in the legality of their position." He also says that it is a mistake to play at revolt. "It is but poor propaganda to behave like a dog sniffing at a red hot poker, and being obliged to draw his nose back in a hurry for fear of being burnt." So, he repeats, "our sole business is to make Socialists."

In 1888, two years before he was driven out of the League, he wrote to Bruce Glasier, a Scotch Socialist friend, defining his position:

"1st. Under no circumstances will I give up active propaganda. 2nd. I will make every effort to keep the League together. 3rd. We should treat Parliament as a representative of the enemy. 4th. We might for some definite purpose be forced to send members to Parliament as rebels. 5th. But under no circumstances to help to carry on their government of the country. 6th. And therefore we ought not to put forward palliative measures to be carried through Parliament, for that would be helping them to govern us. 7th. If the League declares for the latter step it ceases to be what I thought it was, and I must try to do what I can outside it. 8th. But short of that I will work inside it."

Soon after this the quarrel came to a head and the Parliamentarians left the League. Of those who remained Morris said:

"One or two are vainglorious humbugs. A good many are men who, poor fellows, owing to their position, cannot argue, and have only impulsive feelings based on no sort of logic, emotional or otherwise, and fall back when there is nothing exciting going on, since they have never had any real grasp of the subject. Many also are so desperately poor that they cannot work much for us... With all this the worst of them are no worse than other people. Mostly they are better, so that supposing we broke up the band, any new band we got together would be composed of just the same elements."

Unfortunately, however, Morris now found himself alone with the Anarchists. "The Anarchist element in us seems determined to drive things to extremity and break us up if we do not declare for Anarchy, which I for one will not do."

During the year of the final quarrel, he writes to Glasier:

"Between you and me the League doesn't get on – except like a cow's tail – downwards. Up here there is now a great deal of quarrelling (in which I take no part), the basis of which is that some of them want the paper made 'more revolutionary,' i.e., they want to write the articles themselves (which they

97. *Bullerswood*, 1889.
   Woven wool carpet on cotton warp,
   764.8 x 398.8 cm.
   Victoria & Albert Museum, London.

98. *Bird and Anemone*, 1881.
   Furnishing fabric. Dyed cotton ground,
   with a block-printed pattern in red madder dye,
   62 x 46 cm.
   Victoria & Albert Museum, London.

99. *St James*, 1881.
   Pattern for silk.
   Victoria & Albert Museum, London.

can't do), and do a little blood and thunder without any meaning, which might get me into trouble, but couldn't hurt them...I am now paying for the League (including paper) at the rate of £500 a year, and I cannot stand it."

But all this, he says, does not trouble him much.

"Socialism is spreading, I suppose on the only lines on which it could spread, and the League is moribund simply because we are outside these lines, as I for one must always be, but I shall be able to do just as much work in the movement when the League is gone as I do now. The main cause of the failure is that you cannot keep a body together without giving it something to do in the present."

At last he was deposed from the editorship of the "Commonweal" and in November 1890 he wrote for the last time in it, speaking of the Socialist movement with sincerity free from all bitterness and a hope free from all illusions.

"Consider, the quality of those who began and carried on this business of reversing the basis of modern society. A few working men, less successful even in the wretched life of labour than their fellows, a sprinkling of the intellectual proletariat, whose keen pushing of Socialism must have seemed pretty certain to extinguish their limited chances of prosperity; one or two outsiders in the game political, a few refugees from the bureaucratic tyranny of foreign governments, and here and there an unpractical, half-cracked artist or author."

Here in the last sentence he was no doubt thinking of himself, half expressing his own opinion, half repealing what others said of him. He knew that he was unpractical to this extent, that he could not give his mind to the business of politics as he had given it to the business of the arts. All his practical work in Socialist agitation had been done against the grain, and done therefore, with only a part of himself. A man cannot be master of any subject unless he gives the whole of himself to it, and Morris had mastered art after art because he had the power of throwing the whole of himself into each of them, even when he was practicing several at the same time. What he had learnt in one helped him in another, but when he came to politics all that he had learnt about the arts was a hindrance rather than a help, for the artist works at his art for its own sake without a thought of further consequences; the politician – and this is the very secret of his craft – always has further consequences on his mind. However disinterested he may be in his general aims, he cannot have the artist's peculiar disinterestedness. He cannot do a job for its own sake and think of nothing but doing it as well as possible. If he does that, he may be a fine orator or a brilliant writer, but he will be a bad politician. Morris knew this well enough, for it was part of his sagacity to understand at once the first principles of any work he undertook. But although he knew it he could not practice it with any joy. He could refrain from insisting upon his own opinion, but he felt ashamed even as he did so. In the article from which I have quoted he says: "Quarrels more than enough we

100. *Orchard Curtain*, c. 1880-1890.

Fabric.

Victoria & Albert Museum, London.

101. *Strawberry-Thief*, 1883.

Printed cotton, 60 x 95.2 cm.

Victoria & Albert Museum, London.

Lo waneth the summer ✤ apple boughs made fair still my garden ✤ Yet twixt sunlight & shade

have had, and sometimes also weak assent for fear of quarrels to what we did not agree with." To him all the contrivance and compromise of the politician seemed weak assent to what he did not agree with, and he felt guilty even while he practiced it from a sense of duty. Indeed, in all his political activity he suffered from a conflict between his sense of duty and the finest of his natural instincts, which proved that he was not born to be a politician. For when a man does what he is born to do his sense of duty is in harmony with the finest of his natural instincts and because of this harmony he can throw the whole of himself into his work. Morris, all through this last statement in the Commonweal expresses a hope which is never affected, but it is really a hope that others will succeed just where he feels that he himself has failed.

> "When I first joined the movement, I hoped that some working-man leader, or rather leaders, would turn up, who would push aside all middle-class help, and become great historical figures. I might still hope for that, if it seemed likely to happen, for indeed I long for it enough; but to speak plainly it does not seem so at present."

There he spoke with perfect honesty, for he had never wished himself to be a leader. His desire had been to obey the orders of some leader that he could trust; and unwillingly he had found himself forced into a kind of leadership from the lack of the great man of the working classes whom he had wished to follow.

Again, he spoke of himself and his own ideas in the following passage:

> "When we first began to work together, there was little said about anything save the great ideals of Socialism, and so far off did we seem from the realisation of these that we could hardly think of any means for their realisation, save great dramatic events which would make our lives tragic indeed, but would take us out of the sordidness of the so-called 'peace' of civilisation. With the great extension of Socialism this also is changed. Our very success has dimmed the great ideals that first led us on, for the hope of the partial and, so to say, vulgarised realisation of Socialism is now pressing on us... Methods of realisation, therefore, are now more before our eyes than ideals, but it is of no use talking about methods which are not, in part at least, immediately feasible, and it is of the nature of such partial methods to be sordid and discouraging, though they may be necessary."

That phrase "the vulgarised realisation of Socialism" betrays the artist in politics against his will. He knew that the realisation must be inferior to the idea, but the true politician, however high-minded, sacrifices something of the idea with joy for the sake of the realisation. The artist cannot do this. He judges politics as if they were art, and in speaking of vulgarised realisation he uses an artistic metaphor to describe what would be a failure in art though it may be a success in politics. That was why Morris felt that he himself must always be outside the lines on which

102. *Bird and Anemone*, 1881.
Printed cotton, design produced as a wallpaper and a chintz.

103. **Edward Burne-Jones** (for the design) and
Morris & Co. (for the production),
The Romaunt of the Rose:
The Heart of the Rose, c. 1890.
High warp tapestry, wool and silk weft on
cotton warp, 150 x 201 cm.
Badisches Landesmuseum, Karlsruhe.

Socialism could be realised; but his experience had not disgusted him either with himself or with other Socialists. It had only made him see more clearly how he could best work for Socialism. He had done his duty as a private. He had spoken at street corners, had been in conflict with the police and had learnt from the riots of 1886 and 1887, if he needed to learn it, that a revolution at present was impossible, and that even if the impossible happened, the rebels would not know what to do with their success. From then on he continued to work hard, but without the feverish earnestness of one who felt something must be done at once to save the world. From the patient endurance of disappointments and injustice he had acquired a more tranquil faith, in its nature like the faith of those who believe that the process of the Universe will justify itself in a future state. At first, with no belief of his own in a life after death, he had fought against present evils fiercely and wildly like a rat in a corner, but the fever was cured by the very process of fighting, and though his dogmatic beliefs may not have changed, he obtained the spiritual rest of one who has done his duty. He had not laboured to obtain it, but it came to him like a happy physical weariness in the evening of his life.

Morris and those who left the League with him formed another society of their own called the *Hammersmith Socialist Society*. "I feel twice the man since I have spoken out," he wrote. "I dread a quarrel above all things, and I have had this one on my mind for a year or more. But I am glad it is over at last, for in good truth I would about as soon join a White Rose Society as an Anarchist one, such nonsense as I deem the latter." The new society had evening lectures every Sunday in a lecture hall that had once been the stable of Kelmscott House. Men such as Stepniak, John Burns, Bernard Shaw, Lord Haldane, Sidney Webb, and Walter Crane gave lectures. Morris himself would take the chair and sit at a plain wooden table taking notes or decorating the paper with flowers and lettering. Miss May Morris tells us:

> "When the meeting was over, Mr. Walker, or one of us, would often go to the chairman's table just to see what the little drawings were, left on paper or blotting-pad. Such drawings – dream-roses and twining garlands that formed themselves unbidden; at times, maybe, a mechanical aid through certain moments of weariness when some member of the audience is dealing with a misapprehended aspect of economics with which he bores the others almost to tears."

Morris still continued to speak out of doors on Sunday mornings at Hammersmith or in other places about London, and he grew more hopeful of a general enlightenment and a general spread of Socialist ideas even among those who were not Socialists. "The L.C.C.," he wrote, "so far has, to my own experience, shown itself an amazing improvement on the old red-tape public bodies... Of course I don't think much of gas and water Socialism, or indeed of any mere mechanical accessories to Socialism, but I can see that the spirit of the thing is bettering, and in spite of all disappointments I am very hopeful."

In 1893 a united Socialist Committee was formed to publish a manifesto in which the *Social Democratic Federation*, the Fabian Society, and the *Hammersmith Socialist*

104. *Single Stem*, c. 1905.

Colour print from woodblocks.

Victoria & Albert Museum, London.

Society all joined. Shaw says that Morris wrote the draft, but that Hyndman and he, Shaw, could only agree upon the platitudes of the movement. "The result," he adds, "was, I believe, a complete-agreement among the three of us, though we did not formally express it, that the manifesto was beneath contempt." Nothing much came of it, and as Morris had expected nothing he was not disappointed. This was his last public act of any importance. For two years he had had a serious illness, and because of it he had to take care of himself for the years remaining to him. So he passed gradually and quietly out of public life, though he remained the chief of English Socialists, honoured by all, however much they might differ among themselves.

To some this chapter may seem a record of waste and failure, waste of an artist and failure of a politician. However, as a politician Morris's aim was to persuade the world that what he desired was indeed desirable, and the world is not to be persuaded of such things merely by argument or poetry. It can only be convinced that a man does indeed desire what he preaches by the sacrifices that he makes for it. Morris did not make sacrifices to prove the strength of his desire, but the strength of his desire forced him to make them. He was driven into action in politics as in art because he could not rest content with mere opinion, and the fact that he was less gifted as a politician than as an artist only proved the force of his passion. He may not have been exceptionally persuasive to the crowds that gathered at street corners to hear him preach, but his writings are more persuasive because he did so. His business was not so much to argue as to bear witness, and his sacrifice was part of his testimony.

Many who admire him as an artist think that when he became a politician he was a dreamer walking in his sleep and treading in dangerous places. But whatever he may have dreamt about the future of men, he had no illusions about their present state. He did not think the poor to be all good or the rich all bad, for if he had thought that he would never have been fool enough to attempt to change the condition of the poor. However fiercely he might talk in moments of exasperation, he was always on the side of reason, order, and peace, and Matthew Arnold himself never pleaded so well for sweetness and light as Morris did in the speech that he delivered over the grave of a poor boy who had been killed in the riots of Bloody Sunday in 1887.

> "Our friend who lies here, has had a hard life and met with a hard death; and if society had been differently constituted his life might have been a delightful, a beautiful, and a happy one. It is our business, to begin to organise for the purpose of seeing that such things shall not happen, to try to make this earth a beautiful and happy place."

Every one now knows that this world is less beautiful and happy than it might be. We have all lost the Victorian complacency that was not like despair. We do not believe in the mechanical action of progress or that our civilisation has been freed forever from the peril and beauty of the past. We know that it can only be preserved from peril and restored to beauty by the constant exercise of our own wills. We have both a conviction of sin and a hope of salvation, and we owe both to William Morris more than to any other single man.

105. **Dante Gabriel Rossetti**,
Ecce Ancilla Domini! (The Annunciation), 1850.
Oil on canvas, 73 x 42 cm.
Tate Gallery, London.

106. **Walter Crane**, *Neptune's Horses*, 1892.
Oil on canvas, 86 x 215 cm.
Neue Pinakothek, Munich.

Maturity and Assertion

The Prose Romances and Later Poems

Only two of Morris's prose romances are as well known as they deserve, the *Dream of John Ball* and *News from Nowhere*; they are well known because of their political purpose. They tell us directly and eloquently what Morris most valued in life, and the *Dream of John Ball* is also a vivid picture of a time which he knew almost as well as if he had lived in it.

His other romances have no political intention, though he began to write them when he was still fiercely occupied with politics. The first of them, *The House of the Wolfings*, was begun early in 1888, and *The Roots of the Mountains* followed it the next year. Both have more contact with reality than the five later romances in that they are on the borderland of history. *The House of the Wolfings* is a story of Goths in conflict with the Romans when the power of Rome was beginning to decline. The Romans appear in it much as they appear in the story of Cymbeline. It is a legend told from the standpoint of the Goths. *The Roots of the Mountains* is a tale of the same people but later in date, for now they are fighting with the Huns, not the Romans; at least we may presume the Dusky Men, whom they overcome, to be Huns. We may also guess that in writing those two tales Morris was stealing a holiday from his political work and yet remembering it.

The Goths in both are people he loves, the people who made the art of the Middle Ages and who destroyed that Roman Power he detested. In each book they fight a simple fight with baser enemies, and no doubt, as he wrote, Morris wished that his own fight was as simple. He said that he enjoyed writing *The Roots of the Mountains* more than any other of his books, and he took pleasure in describing the ritual and custom of the people, which some leaders may not have shared. The book contains one of the finest fights in literature; it is not merely a battle of two barbarous tribes, but a conflict between promise and destruction.

Morris wrote this not out of blood lust but because he knew that such a conflict is constantly being waged somewhere in the world, whether openly or covertly. He makes his readers feel this fight to be as momentous and a victory as glorious as Marathon. The truth of history was never made so romantic in any historical novel as it is here in the first signs and threats of the Dusky men. The story is told not as a modern historian might tell it, but as it might have been experienced in the ignorance and uncertainty of the time. Morris plunged into the past not merely to make a story, but because he enjoyed living in it, because he had the power thus to take a holiday from the present.

107. *Musical Angels* (detail), 1869.
Stained glass window.
St Michael's Church, Tilehurst, Berkshire.

108. *Musical Angels* (detail of the upper half
the *Angels Window*), 1869.
Stained glass window.
St Michael's Church, Tilehurst, Berkshire.

The House of the Wolfings is less coherent than The Roots of the Mountains, and the mixture of prose and poetry makes it less easy to read for those who would have their reading made easy. Yet it contains poetry and that alone ought to make it celebrated. The poetry and the prose are most beautiful where the story has magic like that in the later romances. Here is the speech of the Wood-Sun, a kind of Undine, to her earthly lover Thiodolf:

> Thou sayest it: I am outcast; for a god that lacketh mirth
> Hath no more place in Godhome and never a place on earth.
> A man grieves, and he gladdens, or he dies and his grief is gone;
> But what of the grief of the gods, and the sorrow never undone?
> Yea verily I am the outcast. When first in thine arms I lay,
> On the blossoms of the woodland my godhead passed away.

This has the music which Morris alone of our modern poets has made, the music of folksong enriched but not robbed of its freshness, as if it were transferred from a lonely flute to all instruments without suffering by the change.

The rest of the romances were published in the following order: The Glittering Plain, The Wood beyond the World, The Well at the World's End, The Water of the Wondrous Isles, and The Sundering Flood. Morris seems to have written them as he told tales in his boyhood, purely for the pleasure of it. They belong to no time or place and are like no other tales in English literature. He began one or two of them in verse and then gave it up, perhaps because his energy had slackened with all his labours. Indeed, he wrote them, as Shakespeare wrote his last romances, with all the case of mastery but more lazily than Sigurd. And yet they seem to me more imaginative than most of the stories of The Earthly Paradise, for in all of them he writes as if he knew the strange world that he describes down to the smallest particular. They have been called vague, and yet one of their chief merits is the clearness of every detail described. They are remote, but they are not unreal, for Morris himself lived in them as he wrote them. They may be impossible, but they are not incredible; for Morris, though he did not believe in actual magic, could write of it as if he did, and his enchantresses seem to be, not mere beautiful bogies, but symbols of the real mystery of alluring evil. And his characters, however simply drawn, are living men and women. Indeed, now and again he draws them with a subtlety which will surprise those who think that he took no interest in human beings. He had himself a strong turn for introspection, but seems to have regarded it as a bad habit; at least he often cut introspective passages out of his poetry; and sometimes he reveals in these romances what introspection had taught him. It is easy enough for any one who has never read them to enumerate their defects; and in theory perhaps they ought to be as empty as they are said to be. But in practice they are not empty, for the story in each is enthralling; and also because it happens in a world rendered vividly real and beautiful. No one ever described country better or weaved descriptions more artfully into a story than Morris. Thus the desert in

109. **Philip Webb**, **William Morris** and **Edward Burne-Jones**, The Creation, 1861.
Stained glass window.
All Saints Church, Selsley, Gloucestershire.

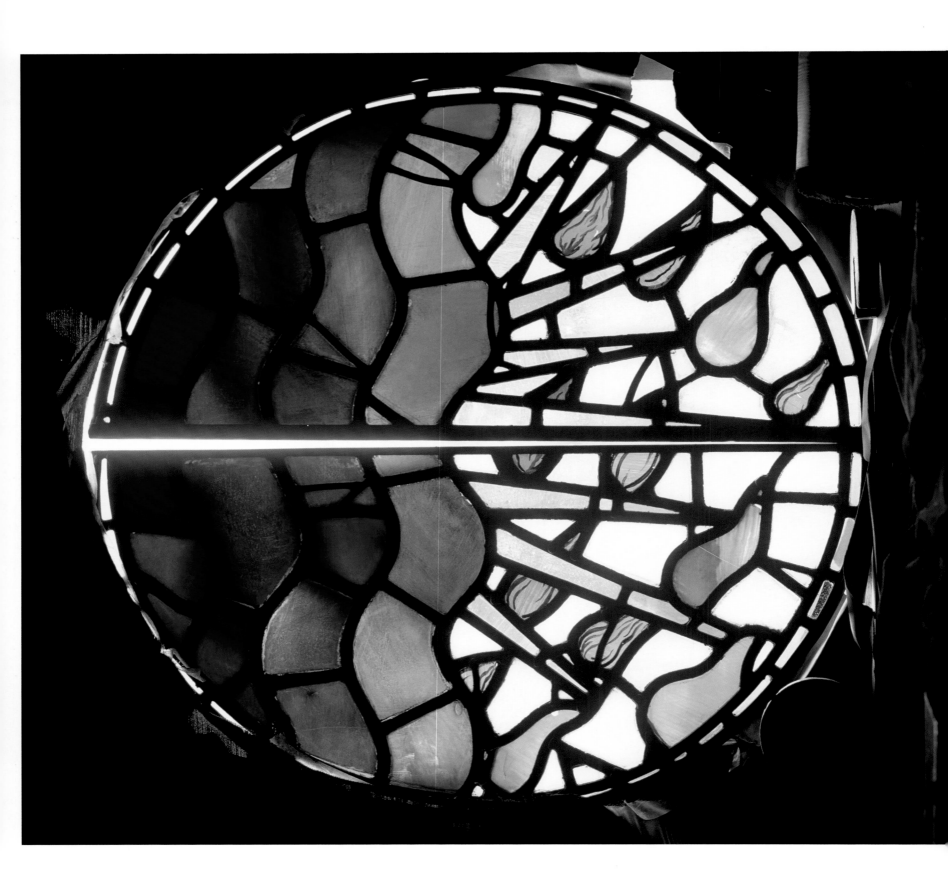

The Glittering Plain is drawn from Iceland, and the country of *The Well at the World's End* from the hills and meadows round Kelmscott Manor. There are journeys in all these stories as in all good romances; and, whatever strange adventures may occur in them, they pass through a country we see with our own eyes. And when Morris brings the hero to a city, it is always a city of the Middle Ages, which he describes as wonderfully and delightfully as he imagines it himself. The Middle Ages as he describes them are not fantastic; they are hardly even romantic, as the word is commonly used. Rather, they are classical, for their art was the classical art to Morris, and he makes us feel that we could live in those cities without finding them strange or barbarous.

One charge has been brought against him more often than any other, namely that he wrote Wardour Street English. This implies that his romances were forgeries of some old style like the buildings of the Gothic revival. Now it is true that Morris had a taste for a few obsolete words and constructions. That was one of his whims, but he used these words and constructions because he liked them, not because he was trying to imitate any old writings. His language, like his stories, is not an imitation of anything; and, except for a few words, it is far easier to understand, because it has more precise meaning than most leading articles. Someone who cannot read these romances because now and again he comes upon a word like *braithly* or *kenspeckle* or *yea-said,* must be like the princess who could not sleep a wink because there was a pea under the forty mattresses of her bed. If Morris had been an affected writer he would have betrayed his affectation in his style; whereas, except for these few whims, he is the simplest writer of his time. Indeed, his strangest constructions are simpler than those to which we are accustomed; and I am, perhaps, unjust to him when I speak of them as whims. He was so used to them himself that he may not have known that they would sound strange to his readers. He may have used them and his outlandish words merely because he was trying to write as well as he could, and therefore used every means that he could find, out of his vast, knowledge of English new and old, to express his meaning as simply as possible. It is true that he does not use these words or constructions in his lectures, but every writer varies to some extent with his subject matter, and Morris varied more than most, because he had a greater mastery and knowledge of English. The main objection to the use of strange words or constructions is that it distracts the reader's attention from the meaning in which it is expressed. One soon gets used to Morris's oddities, whereas the oddities of affectation can never be ignored, since they are assumed to attract notice.

Stevenson once wrote a letter to Morris, which he never sent, protesting against his use of "whereas" for "where". But he protested as an admirer who did not wish to have his admiration lessened by any trifle. "For the love of God," he wrote: "My dear and honoured Morris, use where, and let us know whereas we are, wherefore our gratitude shall grow, whereby you shall be the more honoured wherever men use clear language, whereas now, although we honour, we are troubled."

110. **William Morris** or **Edward Burne-Jones**,
Light and Darkness, Night and Day,
(detail from *The Creation*), 1861.
Stained glass window.
All Saints Church, Selsley, Gloucestershire.

But those who accuse Morris of writing Wardour Street English do not honour him, and betray their ignorance not only of his genius but also of his character. Living as he did, when the great mass of men thought art a thing of no importance, and desiring above all things to make them see that it was important, he was inclined in his own work to be too consciously artistic, as good men in a time of general immorality are inclined to be too consciously moral. Just as he saw machine-made ornament everywhere around him, so he saw the English language in newspapers and books used without simplicity or beauty or precision. So when he used it himself, and especially when he used it in his prose romances, he was anxious to purify it of pompous and stale ugliness acquired through misuse. He had a dislike, perhaps unreasonable, for rhetoric, very like Renaissance floridity of ornament, which the Elizabethans introduced into our literature. For him Chaucer was the perfect master of style in poetry, and in his prose romances he tried to write like a prose Chaucer, not slavishly imitating him, but consciously avoiding the more vague and laboured beauties of later English. He did this without difficulty, for his own mind, when untroubled, worked as easily and simply as the mind of any medieval storyteller, and his own natural interests were medieval rather than modern. That was what he meant when he said that he was born out of due time.

But, unlike Chaucer, he had to avoid many literary habits of his own time, and he found he could do this most easily by establishing a prose convention of his own. In his early prose stories he had not yet established it, and the style in them is often incongruous with the subject. But in the later romances it has become natural to him, so natural that he is never hampered by it, and indeed hardly conscious of it. It is not a style in which the greatest things could be said, but these romances do not aim at the greatest things. Nor do we feel the want of the greatest things in them, or feel the writer has attempted more than he could. The style itself helps to make that beautiful world so complete, far from the reality of our experience. It is not so much archaic as romantic; it is a language freed, as the stories themselves are freed, from all associations with modern ugliness.

In those stories Morris was giving himself his last romantic holiday, and we too can take a romantic holiday in reading them, if we are content to enjoy their sweetness without longing for modern spices. They are stories for grown-up children, such as Morris himself remained through all the labours and troubles of his later years. These gave him wisdom and a new passion of thought, but they did not destroy his simplicity or that purity of palate, like a child's, for which the primitive pleasures of life remained the best.

111. **William Morris** or **Edward Burne-Jones**,
Heaven, Earth and Water,
(detail from *The Creation*), 1861.
Stained glass window.
All Saints Church, Selsley, Gloucestershire.

Morris wrote little poetry in his later years, but in the *Commonweal* he published a narrative poem of modern life called *The Pilgrims of Hope*, which has been privately reprinted in England and published in a pirated edition in America. Morris himself only included three numbers of it, *The Message of the March Wind*, *Mother and Son*, and *The Half of Life Gone*, in the collection of his later poems

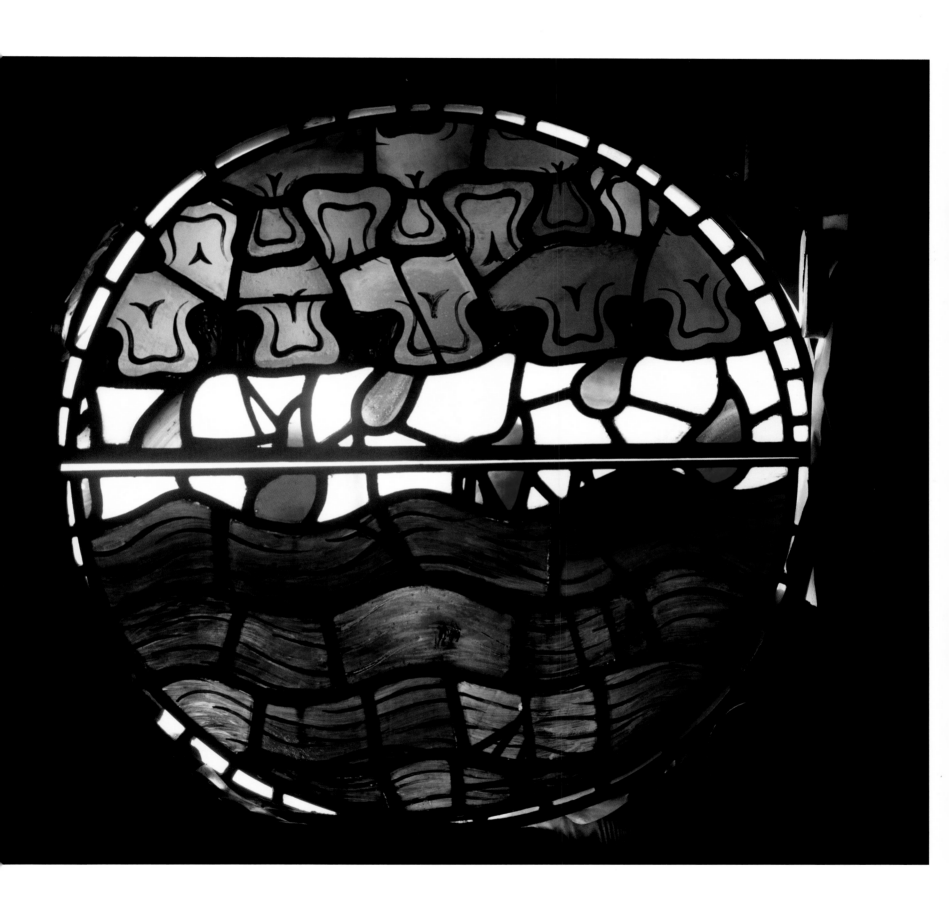

112. *Musical Angels* (detail of the lower
half of the *Angel Window*), 1869.
Stained glass window.
St Michael's Church, Tilehurst, Berkshire.

113. **Edward Burne-Jones**, *Liberty*, c. 1886.
Cartoon for a window at Manchester College
Chapel, Oxford.
Black and white chalk, 138.4 x 47 cm.
Private collection.

114. **Edward Burne-Jones**, *Liberty*, 1898.
Stained glass window, 191.6 x 48.3 cm.
Unitarian Chapel, Heywood Lancashire.

which he published in 1891 under the title *Poems by the Way*. These are his masterpieces of lyrical poetry. The rest of the poem, though unequal, is as exciting to read as any novel, and often rises to extreme beauty. It is easy to find weak lines in it, but the weakest usually lead to some passage of sudden glory that would be less glorious if it were not so introduced. Most of the poem is in the metre of *Sigurd*, and Morris could not lower the excitement of that metre to suit his more prosaic passages. These sometimes sound, therefore, like reciter's poetry, but are far better verse than the prosaic passages of Maud; however weak in themselves, they help tell the story.

As a whole the poem is a lonely triumph in modern literature in that it has all the thrill of new ideas and fresh experience, and yet is for the most part high poetry. It is the story of a man and a woman who love each other and become Socialists, and in *The Message of the March Wind*, the man speaks to the woman in the first happiness of their love:

> From township to township, o'er down and by tillage,
> Far, far have we wandered and long was the day,
> But now cometh eve at the end of the village,
> Where over the gray wall the church riseth gray.

The rest and beauty of the hour possess them, but their happiness makes them feel all the more sharply the misery of the London poor:

> This land we have loved in our love and our leisure .
> For them hangs in heaven, high out of their reach;
> The wide hills o'er the sea-plain for them have no pleasure,
> The gray homes of their fathers no story to teach.

There Morris is speaking for himself, speaking as if his own new pity were heightened by youth and the glory of first love; and indeed it is the greatest triumph of the poet to recover his youth in the art of his later years and to present the lessons of experience as if he had learnt them as he once learnt to love. So the hope of love and the hope of the world become almost one to the mind of this lover and he makes one music of them both:

> Like the seed of midwinter, unheeded, unperished,
> Like the autumn-sown wheat 'neath the snow lying green,
> Like the love that o'ertook us, unawares and uncherished,
> Like the babe 'neath thy girdle that groweth unseen;
> So the hope of the people now buddeth and groweth,
> Rest fadeth before it, and blindness and fear;
> It biddeth us learn all the wisdom it knoweth;
> It hath found us, and held us, and biddeth us hear.

In *Mother and Son* the babe is born, and the mother talks to it alone in London by night of its father and herself, and of how they came to love each other, and of the faith he has taught her. Tolstoy himself could not have made her tell more of the secrets of her heart; but Morris makes her tell them in poetry that is like a folk-song of our own time: Lo, amidst London I lift thee,

And how little and light thou art,
And thou without hope or fear
Thou fear and hope of my heart!
Lo, here thy body beginning,
O son, and thy soul and thy life;
But how will it be if thou livest,
And enterest into the strife,
And in love we dwell together
When the man is grown in thee,
When thy sweet speech I shall hearken,
And yet 'twixt thee and me
Shall rise that wall of distance,
That round each one doth grow,
And maketh it hard and bitter
Each other's thought to know.

She tells him what kind of woman she is and how she has lived and grown to beauty, and all in language as simple as the simplest prose, which makes its own music as if it were the first poetry ever written:

Now to thee alone will I tell it
That thy mother's body is fair,
In the guise of the country maidens
Who play with the sun and the air;
Who have stood in the row of the reapers
In the August afternoon,
Who have sat by the frozen water
In the high day of the moon,
When the lights of the Christmas feasting
Were dead in the house on the hill,
And the wild geese gone to the saltmarsh
Had left the winter still.

Through all that long practice of verse and storytelling, through all that love of old romance, Morris at last had attained to this, that he could make a new story as beautiful as an old one and new music which seems a happy chance of the words falling together. Here the woman tells how she left her home in the early morning:

All things I saw at a glance;
The quickening fire-tongues leapt
Through the crackling heap of sticks,
And the sweet smoke up from it crept,
And close to the very hearth
The low sun flooded the floor,
And the cat and her kittens played
In the sun by the open door.
The garden was fair in the morning,
And there in the road he stood
Beyond the crimson daisies
And the hush of southernwood.

Then she is proud of their love and tells her son, the fruit of it, everything that she hopes for him and for the future:

But sure from the wise and the simple
Shall the mighty come to birth;
And fair were my fate, beloved,
If I be yet on the earth
When the world is awaken at last,
And from mouth to mouth they tell
Of thy love and thy deeds and thy valour,
And thy hope that nought can quell.

In *The Half of Life Gone* she is dead, and the man remembers her as he watches the haymaking and speaks as if with her music:

Lo now! the woman that stoops
And kisses the face of the lad,
And puts a rake in his hand
And laughs with his laughing face.
Whose is the voice that laughs
In the old familiar place?
Whose should it be but my love's,
If my love were yet on the earth?
Could she refrain from the fields
Where my joy and her joy had birth?

He falls into grief at the memory, but checks it with a pride in his own past joy and even in the sharpness of his present sorrow:

O fool, what words are these?
Thou hast a sorrow to nurse,

115. **Edward Burne-Jones** (for the design) and
Morris & Co. (for the production),
Musical Angels (detail), 1882.
Stained glass window.
Church of St Peter and St Paul,
Cattistock, Dorset.

116. **Dante Gabriel Rossetti**, *Venus Verticordia*,
1864-1868.
Oil on canvas, 98 x 70 cm.
Russel-Cotes Art Gallery and Museum,
Bournemouth.

And thou hast been bold and happy;
But these if they utter a curse,
No sting it has and no meaning,
It is empty sound on the air.
Thy life is full of mourning,
And theirs so empty and bare,
That they have no words of complaining;
Nor so happy have they been
That they may measure sorrow
Or tell what grief may mean.

Here Morris speaks again himself, though he had never known the grief of which he speaks. He thought, no doubt, of his own good fortune as a mere chance, and he was so concerned with the well-being of the world at large that he could not be satisfied with that chance happiness and tried to imagine how he would face life without it. It is out of such thoughts that poets create tragedies, even when they themselves have all the happiness that life can give. They are not discontented with their happiness, but they cannot lose themselves in it because it is not part of the common lot of men or inevitable, like birth and death. In thought, at any rate, they must make trial of that unhappiness which is no less common. And the sense of this grows on them with years so that they become not merely individuals but every man with all human experiences of joy and sorrow. So Morris, when he wrote *The Half of Life Gone*, was speaking for himself as well as for his hero; and the same faculty which enabled him to speak thus of another man's grief as if it were his own made him also feel the wretchedness of the poor as if it were his own. He became a revolutionary because he was a poet and felt his own prosperity to be a mere chance in the present state of his society; just as much as the absence of death in his family. On this point his imagination worked further than any poet's had worked before, but it was still the poetic imagination, in this case driven into politics because he believed that poverty, unlike death, could be abolished by the will of man.

Thus he was able sometimes in his Socialist poems to rise above the level of spirited propagandist verse, as Cowper sometimes rose in his hymns above the level of Hymns Ancient and Modern. *The Day is Coming* begins well enough, but many competent versifiers could have written the first part of it. Then follow verses that only Morris could have written:

But what wealth then shall be left us
When none shall gather gold
To buy his friend in the market,
And pinch and pine the sold?
Nay, what save the lovely city,
And the little house on the hill,

117. **Dante Gabriel Rossetti,**
Dante's Vision of Rachel and Leah, 1855.
Watercolour on paper, 35.2 x 31.4 cm.
Tate Gallery, London.

> And the wastes and the woodland beauty,
> And the happy fields we till;
> And the homes of ancient stories,
> The tombs of the mighty dead;
> And the wise men seeking out marvels,
> And the poet's teeming head;
> And the painter's hand of wonder;
> And the marvelous fiddle-bow,
> And the banded choirs of music:
> All those that do and know.

That music, so clear, so sudden, transforming the words the moment he begins to speak of what he loves, reveals to us the poet in the politician and shows us that it was the poet's desire which turned him to politics so that he might, if he could, create what he desired. These poems of his last volume are not much known, but the best of them seem to me, even when I remember *Sigurd*, to prove that he never did in poetry all that he might have done. That great effort of his later years, to be the poet in action, to remould the world itself nearer to his heart's desire, overtaxed even his strength. For a moment, in *Mother and Son*, he was able to make a saga out of the present, to see the conflict of his own time as if it were a war of gods and giants. But he had not energy enough to do this for more than a moment. His body, though not his genius, was growing old. The great inspiration of his life came too late, and when he turned away from politics he took his rest in labours that would have been heavy for any other man, but for him were only a pastime.

Later Years and Character

In the spring of 1891, when Morris was fifty-seven years old, his body began to warn him that he had overtaxed it. He fell ill of the gout, complicated by weakness of the kidneys.

"My hand seems lead and my wrist string," he wrote to a friend; and he was told that in future he must always take great care of himself. After this illness he lived more than five years and they were crowded with various labours; but the chief work of his life was done and every year he was a little weaker. Yet his autumn was a season of mellow fruitfulness and he seems to be writing of it in that poem which he made to be embroidered on the hanging of his bed.

> The wind's on the wold
> And the night is a cold.
> And Thames runs chill
> 'Twixt mead and hill.
> But kind and dear
> Is the old house here

118. **József Rippl-Rónai**, *Woman in Red*, 1898.
Embroidered tapestry.
Museum of Applied Arts, Budapest.

And my heart is warm
Midst winter's harm.
Rest then and rest,
And think of the best
'Twixt summer and spring,
When all birds sing
In the leaves of the tree,
And ye lie in me
And scarce dare move,
Lest earth and its love
Should fade away
E'er the full of the day.
I am old and have seen
Many things that have been;
Both grief and peace
And wane and increase.
No fate I tell
Of ill or well,
But this I say,
Night treadeth on day,
And for worst and best
Right good is rest.

It was before this illness that he made his translation of the *Odyssey*, but it may be spoken of here as one of the labours of his later years. Like the prose romances it has never had the fame it deserves because of the outlandish words he sometimes uses in it. He succeeded with it far better than with the *The Aeneid*, because Homer, unlike Virgil, was a great storyteller, and Morris, whatever else he has lost, has kept the momentum and excitement of the story better than any other translator. His translation is rough and odd at times. He himself said that, it was too like Homer for the public to take to it – but it reads as if it were an original poem written for the sake of the story; and it is always best in the great places. Here, for instance, is the passage at the end of the twenty-first book where Odysseus bends the bow:

Then straight, as a man well learnèd in the lyre and the song
On a new pin tightly stretcheth the cord and maketh fast
From side to side the sheep-gut welltwined and overcast:
So the mighty bow he bendeth with no whit of labouring,
And caught it up in his right hand, and fell to try the string,
That 'neath his hand sang lovely as a swallow's voice is fair.

119. Adjustable-Back Chair, upholstered in original
Bird woollen tapestry, 1870-1890.
Ebonized wood with Utrecht Velvet upholstery.
Loose covers of wool tapestry,
97.8 x 71.1 x 91.4 cm.
Victoria & Albert Museum, London.

Here, as elsewhere, Morris deals with the technical details as if he knew their detail, not as if he were a scholar painfully doing his best with them, and since the

Maturity and Assertion

Odyssey is full of technical details and Homer clearly took great delight in them, Morris's power of treating them like a craftsman gives to his translation a reality which is not to be found in any other. It is not "a pretty poem" perhaps, but it is as near to Homer as we are likely to get in English until another master of narrative poetry as great as Morris chooses to spend some years of his life upon a translation.

To Morris himself the *Odyssey* was only one of many books that he wished to translate. For him, Greek art and literature did not possess the pre-eminence they have for many artists and men of letters. He would admit that the Greeks had a greater power of execution than any other people known to us; but, he would have said, they never conceived a building like St Sophia or a story like that of the *Volsunga* saga. He saw all their works naked of the enormous prestige which they have in the modern world and enjoyed them in his own way and as if he had discovered them for himself. So he turned from the *Odyssey* to the translation of Early French romances and to a metrical version of Beowulf, and he enjoyed printing these things at his press as much as he enjoyed translating them. Indeed, he worked at the press as if he were a young man just starting upon business, and the letters of his last years are full of hopes and fears about the great *Kelmscott Chaucer* which was published a few months before he died. He was very angry with the holidays of the last Easter he lived through, because they delayed the printing of the Chaucer. "Four mouldy Sundays in a mouldy row," he wrote, "the press shut and Chaucer at a standstill." But, though he still lectured and did much work for the *Society for the Protection of Ancient Buildings* and wrote his prose romances, he was, by comparison with his own past, gradually withdrawing from active life. In 1895 he said to Burne-Jones: "The best way of lengthening out the rest of our days now is to finish our old things." A change had been coming over him for some time, Lady Burne-Jones says, "which we tried to think was nothing beyond the usual effect of time." At the beginning of 1896 Burne-Jones began to be seriously troubled by signs of weakness he observed, and the nature of these signs shows us what his vitality had been. "Last Sunday," Burne-Jones writes, "in the very middle of breakfast, Morris began leaning his forehead on his hand, as he does so often now. It is a thing I have never seen him do before in all the years I have known him." In 1895 he had begun to suffer from sleeplessness and when he could not sleep he would get up and work at *The Sundering Flood*. In January 1896 he went to a meeting of the *Society for the Protection of Ancient Buildings* for the last time. A friend, walking away from it with him, noticed his weakness and said that it was the worst time of the year. "No it ain't," replied Morris, "it's a very fine time of the year indeed. I'm getting old, that's what it is." After this he grew weaker very quickly. He was sent to Folkestone for change and, since he got no good by it, his doctor ordered him to take a sea voyage to Norway. This was worse than useless, since he was dying and should have been allowed to die in peace. He was unhappy on the voyage and returned on the 18th of August longing for the quiet of Kelmscott. But he was too ill to go there and never saw that home

120. **Edward Burne-Jones** (for the design), *Ladies and Animals Sideboard*, 1860. Pine painted in oil paint, with gold and silver leaf, 116.8 x 152.4 x 73.7 cm. Victoria & Albert Museum, London.

121. **William Morris**, **Dante Gabriel Rossetti** or **Edward Burne-Jones**, *Untitled*, c. 1860. Four painted panels. Oil on panel, 61 x 41 x 3.2 cm (each). Victoria & Albert Museum, London.

again. His last days were spent in his London house, and there on the 8th of September he dictated the last lines of *The Sundering Flood*, which came to an end without betraying any of the weakness that was overcoming him. In this weakness he was easily moved to tears and wept once when Lady Burne-Jones spoke of the hardships of the poor. Dolmetsch played him some old English music on the virginals but it moved him so much that he could only endure to hear a little of it. He was nursed at the end by Emery Walker and died on the 3rd of October. His disease, a doctor said, "was simply being William Morris, and having done more work than most ten men."

His body was taken to Kelmscott and there buried on the 6th of October. The coffin was carried on a farm wagon from Lechlade station in a storm of wind and rain and was followed by mourners of all classes, both old and young, some of them the friends of his youth, some later followers and admirers. Famous as he was, his death did not make a great stir in the world. At that time only those who knew him knew what posterity would think of him.

Burne-Jones once said of him:

> "There's Morris: the larger half of that wonderful personality will perish when he dies. I've tried to put down or repeat some of his rare sayings, but somehow it always seemed flattish the day after, with all the savour gone out. There is no giving the singularity and the independence of his remarks from anything that went before. What never can be put down are his actions and ways – perpetually walking about a room while he is talking, and his manner of putting his list out to explain the thing to you. When I first knew him at college it was just what it is now."

Some of his old and intimate friends still alive could preserve the legend of him. It is useless for one who never saw him to attempt it or to repeat the old stories of his fits of passion and relentings, of the contrasts between his violence of language and patience of conduct, between his common sense and his dreams. But every one who knew him well has noticed how full of contrasts he was, and yet these contrasts are certainly not the symptoms of any weakening conflict in his character. Morris was a man who had all the prosaic virtues; on one side he might have been the hero of *Tom Brown's School Days*, except that he did not care much for games; on the other he was a visionary who wrote the lyrics of *Love is Enough* and *Think But One Thought of Me Up in the Stars*. Yet those two parts of his nature worked together and none of his friends ever saw any incongruity between them. Perhaps this kind of character is rare in our time only because craftsmen are rare, for the craftsman, if he is to excel, must be both industrious and a visionary, as Morris was. He must have honesty and common sense as well as invention; and his work develops and harmonises both sets of qualities. We shall understand Morris best if we think of him as a craftsman rather

than as a poet, as one who could never see raw material without wishing to make something out of it and who at last saw society itself as a very raw material which set his fingers itching.

Being thus so completely a craftsman he was not, like many poets, absorbed in the intense experience of life nor filled with a devouring curiosity about it. He observed people and things incessantly, but rather as if he knew what could be made out of them than as if he were on a voyage of discovery through life. The world itself was a rough material about which he had made up his mind and, though it might delight or enrage him, it did not greatly surprise him. Thus he made his jokes about it in conversation and in letters, and he had his own peculiar vein of humour; but it was only a pastime to him. He was never enough surprised by life to be humorous in his art. He would criticise people and pass acute judgments upon them, but always by the way. He was not profoundly interested in them any more than in himself. His greatest friends were those with whom he did things, his fellow-workmen like Burne-Jones and Webb and Emery Walker. Indeed, friendship to him meant companionship in work rather than any great intimacy of mind, because he was always working or thinking of his work. He was dependent on nobody, as Burne-Jones remarked, not from any cold-heartedness, but because he always gave more than he received. When he was in a passive mood, he became mysterious, enriching his mind not from other minds but from some source of which he speaks now and again in his poetry. Then he was like a musician listening to melodies that no one else could hear; and all his friends were aware of these withdrawals, more aware, perhaps, than he was himself. To them Morris was a man with a secret of his own which he shared with no one, yet he himself made no mystery about his art or about anything else in his life. He would allow friends to interrupt him in his writing of poetry if he liked to talk with them, knowing that he could go on with his work as soon as the conversation was over. He always talked about art in the most matter-of-fact way, as if it were a job like any other, but there was a kind of reticence in this as in his manner of announcing the birth of his first child to Madox Brown: "Kid having appeared, Mrs. Brown kindly says she will stay till Monday."

Most men who are absorbed in some pursuit like to share their enthusiasm with others, but Morris was quite content with his own enthusiasm and needed no support in that or in anything else. No one was ever less swayed by opinion. If any man can be without vanity, he was without it. He never had any public manners and behaved always as if the world were his workshop and people were there to help or hinder him in his work. His sudden rages were like seizures and they did not affect his intercourse with those who provoked them. If they were signs of hatred at all, it was hatred of ideas or things rather than people, and usually of something that hindered him in his work. Indeed, when he lost his temper with someone, that person had merely become something provoking him, and that, as soon as he recognised the human being again, the rage was over.

He had not the slightest desire to be a gentleman; and the world consisted for him of two classes, those who could make things and those who could not. Among the latter were money-makers and middlemen of all kinds, including the great mass of the professional classes; and these he despised and pitied much as a good-natured athletic schoolboy will despise and pity those of his schoolfellows who are no good at games. Morris became angry with them, and expressed his anger in strong language, only when he found that they had power over those who could make things. Then he called them smoke-dried swindlers and other things, but he would have been quite kind to them, as he was kind to all the incompetent, if they had been in their proper places. He knew, of course, that he himself had extraordinary powers, but he was no more proud of them than a well-bred nobleman is proud of his rank. He did not think of himself as a privileged person at all, and, if he snubbed any one, it was because he was angry, not to assert his own dignity. Mackail tells us that one of his intimate friends spoke of his "childlike shamelessness" as his deepest quality, and one may say, in Whitman's phrase, that he had the "aplomb of animals" and seemed to do everything by instinct and without the misgivings of reason. So his friends could sometimes laugh at him as if he were a delightful and friendly animal, a little puzzled by the criticism of human laughter.

But all this will not explain why his friends loved him or why many who never knew him thought of him as if they had known and loved him. And the effort to explain this brings us to the strongest and deepest contrast in his nature. It has been said that there are two classes of men, the once-born and the twice-born. The once-born are those who seem from first to last at ease with themselves and free from that sense of discord which we call conviction of sin. At their best they give delight to every one with the simplicity and security of their own natures, but there is always some disappointment in their delight. They do all things well, but seem to do them a little too easily and as if there were no possibilities in them beyond their achieve-ment. If one tries to learn their secret, they can tell it no more than if they were animals or flowers. Their well-being seems to be negative as well as positive and the result of a refusal to experience more than will agree with their own temperaments; and because of this refusal they are more delightful in youth than in later years, when they often seem to be superannuated young men and affect us like beautiful women who have never married and keep their virgin beauty a little failed. The twice-born, on the other hand, are not at ease and their youth is often unpleasing because they are full of a sense of discord in themselves. They do not know what they want to be or what they would make of life, and they are restless, imitative and affected. But life is a process of discovery for them and they refuse no experience. They are always in process of making. Sometimes this process is gradual; sometimes it is concentrated in that sudden rebirth which we call conversion. In any case, if they are not wrecked by early inexperience, they improve with years; their very faults change into virtues and they profit from their worst errors. And this happy change in them makes us feel that life is not merely something that happens and is done with, giving good to some and evil to others;

122. **Edward Burne-Jones**,
The Wedding Feast of Sir Devrevaunt, 1860.
One of three wall paintings in the Drawing Room at the Red House, William and Jane Morris modelled for the bride and groom. Victoria & Albert Museum, London.

123. **Edward Burne-Jones**,
Psyche's Wedding, 1895.
Oil on canvas, 119.5 x 215.5 cm.
Musées royaux des Beaux-Arts de Belgique, Brussels.

but that it is an experience, with a purpose beyond itself, by which the least gifted may profit through their very defects.

Now Morris was a man who seemed to have all the simplicity and security of the once-born, and who did everything so easily that he could not be provoked to further effort by his own incompetence. In his earlier years there was nothing to trouble his life of happy activity except the thought that it must some day come to an end. From the first he was afflicted by a pagan fear of death, or rather by the feeling that death, sure to come at last and possible at any moment, made life seem meaningless. He writes of it, now and again in his poetry, like an animal cursed with foreknowledge; it was a fact that he could neither explain nor forget, and he would never allow himself to cherish any hope of a future life. So there was always this dark shadow to the sunlight of his labours; and, however easily he might live, he could not be at ease when he thought of dying. On this point alone he was weaker and less happy than most men, but it was this weakness that saved him from the dangerous contentment of the once-born. How hard he fought against it, we may see from his statement of the northern faith, which I have quoted, and from his saying that a man would be happy if he could hold it and be freed by it from the mist of fear. By the mist of fear he meant that sense of the meaninglessness of life, which haunted his own labours, and he could only regard these as a game to pass the time while life had no meaning for him.

Some men in his case would try to find a meaning in it by thought, but that was not his way, as it was not the way of the northerners whose faith he envied. He could not be persuaded that life had any meaning unless he made it mean something to himself. He could only deliver himself by action, and since society seemed to him to be meaningless and aimless, and so confirmed his fears about life, he fought against these fears by attempting to give society a meaning and an aim.

Now it was the contrast between the once-born, happy Morris, and the Morris born again in this mighty effort, which has turned men's admiration into love. But for that contrast he would have seemed aloof in his good fortune, and other men would have regarded him as the poor regard the rich, both envying and despising them for their ignorance of the hard facts of life. As it is, we can pity Morris besides admiring him, and we can even smile at him as a visionary. He learnt to suffer and to fail like the weakest of us, but suffering and failure came to him not in the ordinary business of life, but when he taxed his strength and wisdom upon a higher business that he chose for himself. Then he, who had won success in so many arts with so much certainty and ease, turned from one hope to another like a bewildered child. He learnt humbly from every disappointment as if he were a clumsy beginner at some poor trade, but whatever else he learnt he would not learn to despair. It seemed to him always that he was doing very little. He never thought of himself as a strong man condescending to work for the weak; and when we read of his labours we too cease to think of him as a great man, as a poet far removed

124. **Philip Webb** (for the design) and **Morris, Marshall, Faulkner & Co.** (for the production), *St George's Cabinet*, 1861. Cabinet with scenes from the life of saint George. Painted and gilded mahogany, pine and oak, with copper mounts, 111 x 178 x 43 cm. Victoria & Albert Museum, London.

125. **Philip Webb** (for the design) and **Morris, Marshall, Faulkner & Co.** (for the production), *St George's Cabinet* (detail of the central panel), 1861. Cabinet with scenes from the life of saint George. Painted and gilded mahogany, pine and oak, with copper mounts, 111 x 178 x 43 cm. Victoria & Albert Museum, London.

126. **Philip Webb** (for the design) and **Morris, Marshall, Faulkner & Co.** (for the production), *St George's Cabinet* (right panel), 1861. Cabinet with scenes from the life of saint George. Painted and gilded mahogany, pine and oak, with copper mounts, 111 x 178 x 43 cm. Victoria & Albert Museum, London.

from us in the immortality of fame. He is one of us when he preaches at street corners with all the music gone from his speech. But it is when we think of him so that we love him, and then he becomes great for us again in the music of those later days, made after he had conquered the fear of death and by his sacrifice, which assured him of life's meaning.

The Ideas of William Morris

Morris clearly expressed his ideas in three books of lectures and essays, *Hopes and Fears for Art*, *Architecture, Industry and Wealth*, and *Signs of Change*; and less directly in his *News from Nowhere*. *News from Nowhere* has always been popular, but the other books are less read than they deserve to be. Morris said that he wrote his lectures with unwilling labour. He did not enjoy the process of thought, but not because he could not think clearly. Indeed, no one has ever written more clearly upon art or upon its relation to the structure of society. It was Ruskin who first taught him to think about this relation; but he had more practical experience of the arts than Ruskin and spoke with a precision and authority due to that experience. In his way, too, he was almost as great a master of prose, and there are passages of eloquence in these books which move us the more because they are so plain in language and so closely connected with his argument.

In nearly all his lectures Morris insists upon this relation between art and the structure of society, and art for him does not mean merely painting and sculpture, but all those works of man in which the workman does better than he is forced to do by his material needs. "Art is man's expression of his joy in labour," he said, and he believed this joy in labour to be the thing best worth having in life. Born into an age of destructive scepticism and himself without belief in any religious dogma, he found in art, in this everlasting effort of man to do better than he need, the most exhilarating mystery of life. The humblest work of art was to him a sign of divinity, a promise of something that he hardly dared believe, and he was moved by it as other men are moved by noble, unexpected actions. For art to him always remained a surprising product of the troubled and laborious life of man, a song of prisoners, as it were, which touched him the more if it was rude and simple.

127. **John Pollard Seddon** (for the design) and
Morris, Marshall, Faulkner & Co.
(for the production),
King René's Honeymoon Cabinet, 1860-1862.
Cabinet decorated with oak, inlaid with
various woods, with painted metalwork and
painted panels, 133.4 x 252 x 87 cm.
Victoria & Albert Museum, London.

128. **Philip Webb** (for the design) and **Morris,
Marshall, Faulkner & Co.**
(for the production), *Armchair*, 1861-1862.
Ebonized wood with gilded bands,
99 x 41 x 43 cm.
Society of Antiquaries of London,
Kelmscott Manor.

129. **Dante Gabriel Rossetti** (for the design) and
Morris & Co. (for the production),
The Rossetti Armchair, 1870-1890.
Ebonized beech, with red painted decoration
and rush seat, 88.8 x 49.5 x 53 cm.
Victoria & Albert Museum, London.

He loved all works of true art not only for the delight they gave him, but also because they seemed to him symptoms of happiness, and he judged a society's happiness by the nature of its art, particularly of the humbler, less conscious, art which beautifies things of ordinary use. He himself began by missing this kind of art in his own time where no one but Ruskin had missed it before. Other men, however less happy they might be for the lack of it, were not aware of its absence, as a man deaf from his birth would be unaware of the pleasure of music, but he from the first was ill at ease, and, when he saw the art of the Middle Ages, he knew what it was that his own day lacked. Then, becoming an artist himself and experiencing the pleasure of art, he saw that in his own day the great mass of men worked without any of that pleasure and that what they made was ugly because it was made without pleasure, or uglier still if with ornament it tried to imitate the happy work of the past. He hated machine-made ornament for its own ugliness, but still more because by its failure it reminded him of what it failed to do. To him it was as sinister as joyless laughter and its prevalence showed that men had forgotten everywhere the very meaning of art, the very desire for that happiness which, he thought, was the best they could have in this life.

Of that happiness he often spoke well, but best perhaps in the lecture upon *Art under Plutocracy*. "The pleasure," he says, "which ought to go with the making of every piece of handicraft has for its basis the keen interest which every healthy man takes in healthy life, and is compounded, it seems to me, chiefly of three elements, variety, hope of creation, and the self-respect which comes of a sense of usefulness; to which must be added that mysterious bodily pleasure which goes with the deft exercise of the bodily powers." Again, addressing an audience of artists, he speaks of it more personally in his lecture on the Beauty of Life.

> "Your pleasure is always with you, nor can you be intemperate in the enjoyment of it, and as you use it, it does not lessen, but grows: if you are by chance weary of it at night, you get up in the morning eager for it; or if perhaps in the morning it seems folly to you for a while, yet presently, when your hand has been moving a little in its wonted way, fresh hope has sprung up beneath it and you are happy again. While others are getting through the day like plants thrust into the earth, which cannot turn this way or that, but as the wind blows them, you know what you want, and your will is on the alert to find it, and you, whatever happens, whether it be joy or grief, are at least alive."

There he spoke out of his own experience, and he could not endure that so few men in our time should share that experience with him. To others the change, through which the mass of men had lost all the happiness of art, seemed as inevitable as a process of nature, but not so to Morris. He believed that the Industrial Revolution had taken men by surprise, that this great power of machinery had come into their hands only to be misused through inexperience.

He believed, too, that a body of false doctrine had grown up to justify that misuse, a kind of religion that denied the will of man and represented civilisation as a mechanical process in which greed of riches was a necessary force. To him civilisation was made by the will of man and greed was a barbaric obstruction to it. Men might will to be rich or they might will to do good work; and there was no irresistible pressure of circumstances to make them choose riches. In *Art under Plutocracy* he shows how the art of the Middle Ages flourished because the craftsman's main object was to do good work, and how gradually the capitalist system grew up and took away from him the power of working for his own customers. He had to work for the capitalist and the capitalist's aim was, not that he should do good work, but that he should make a profit for the capitalist. In the eighteenth century, Morris says, "the idea that the essential aim of manufacture is the making of goods still struggled with a newer idea which has since obtained complete victory, namely, that it is carried on for the sake of making a profit for the manufacturer on the one hand, and on the other for the employment of the working classes." In fact, as he puts it, we think of commerce as an end in itself and not as a means. That is our great error, and it is one which we have chosen to make for ourselves and need not make any longer. There is nothing inevitable in the capitalist with his tyranny over both producer and consumer; that is merely one of the many tyrannies to which men have submitted, and it will seem as absurd to future ages as any oriental despotism seems to us.

But all these tyrannies are submitted to because the mass of men take them for granted, and they are first threatened when some man refuses to take them for granted and sees that they exist merely because men submit to them. Morris was such a man. He, with his great knowledge of the past, saw that this tyranny of the capitalist was a new thing, an unhappy accident of our time, and long before he became a Socialist he began his rebellion against it. His own aim from the first was to be a free workman, to find his own customers and to do good work for them. He saw clearly enough that he could never have had this freedom if he had not been himself a capitalist. Without his fortune he would have had to obey some capitalist or starve. The only craftsmen, of his time or ours, who keep the craftsman's freedom are painters and sculptors; and that is the reason why nearly all men who wish to be artists become painters or sculptors, and why there are far too many pictures and works of sculpture produced. Morris, then, made use of his capital to purchase his freedom; but his wish was that all men should be freeborn. His own motive, as a capitalist, was not to make goods for a profit, but to do good work and to find buyers for it; and, having this motive, he cannot be reproached as being himself that which he denounced. Indeed, those who reproach him so take no account of the history of his mind. He began merely with a desire for his own freedom, which he obtained by the only means possible to him, and it was his experience of the blessings of this freedom that made him so ardently desire it for others.

130. **Morris & Co.**,
Settee from the Sussex Range, c. 1865.
Ebonized beech and rush seat,
85.1 x 137.2 x 41 cm.
William Morris Gallery, London.

He proved, with the success of his own firm, that there was still a public that desired good work, and the proof was the foundation of his hope that a right relation might again be established between producer and consumer. We cannot understand the growth of his ideas unless we realise that they all grew out of his own experience as a workman. He was never a theorist and he was not accustomed to thinking in terms of political economy. For him the social problem was not one of the distribution of wealth. It was always a problem of the relations between producer and consumer. There was, he held, a natural desire in man to do good work and a desire, equally natural, to obtain it. In a well-ordered society both these desires would be fulfilled and every one would profit by them both. In his own society he found that they were commonly not fulfilled because of the interference of the capitalist, who made the producer work for his profit and who forced goods made for profit on the consumer. Thus, to him the capitalist was merely a nuisance who prevented the producer from making what he wanted to make and the consumer from buying what he wanted to buy; he was a man who had perverted the energies of mankind to serve his own ends.

If this was not so, why, he asked, had the enormous increase in productive power so little increased the general prosperity?

> "Why have our natural hopes been so disappointed? Surely because in these latter days, in which as a matter of fact machinery has been invented, it was by no means invented with the aim of saving the pain of labour. The phrase labour-saving machinery is elliptical, and means machinery which saves the cost of labour, not the labour itself, which will be expended, when saved, on tending other machines."

In fact, machinery is used for the profit of the man who owns it, that is to say the capitalist, and for that reason it is constantly misused. Morris himself had no blind hatred of machinery. Rightly used, he saw that it would make the burden of necessary drudgery so much lighter that men would have more leisure than they have ever had for the work in which they can take pleasure. That is what we might expect to happen in an age of great mechanical advance. But it has not happened because we do not use machinery to lighten the burden of labour. It is not a power in the hands of society at all, but a power in the hands of the capitalist, by means of which he makes a profit out of society.

All this cannot be denied; the only question is whether it is inevitable, and Morris could not believe that it was inevitable. He thought that a society could organise itself to obtain what it wanted, and that the prevalence of high or base desires determined its structure. Here, like Ruskin, he was in direct opposition to the orthodox political economists of his time, who held that the social structure, unlike the political, was imposed upon men by circumstances and in particular by what they called the laws of supply and demand. In answer to that Morris said that men

131. **Edward Burne-Jones** and **Kate Faulkner** (for the design) and **John Broadwood** (for the production), Grand Piano, 1883. Oak, stained and decorated with gold and silver-gilt gesso, 266 x 140.5 x 45.7 cm. Victoria & Albert Museum, London.

would demand what they wanted, and that, if they demanded it bravely enough, they could get it. The present structure of society existed because they demanded riches without knowing clearly what they wished to do with them. This demand was not in the least inevitable; it was merely the result of stupidity and fear. If only men could be brought to see that riches in our present state of society can purchase little that is worth having, if only they could be brought to see what is worth having, the nature of their demand will change, and with it the supply.

Morris himself, by reason of his own great gifts and of the experience that he had gotten from the exercise of them, knew well what was worth having in life; and his real objective, in all his political activities, was to communicate this knowledge to other men. If they desired what he desired, they would demand what he demanded, and the structure of society would change in accordance with their demands. This was not mere imperious egotism on his part. He knew that he himself had been fortunate in his gifts and in the fact that he was born rich enough to exercise them freely, but he believed that nearly all men could enjoy the happiness he got, if only they had the chance to do so. And he went among them to tell them what this natural and wholesome happiness was, and by what means they were prevented from experiencing it.

His lecture on *Art and Socialism* is in the main a description of men's present slavery to commerce, and an exhortation to them to free themselves from it. The present famine of art, as he calls it, is only one effect of that slavery, but it was the effect which he himself felt most bitterly and which seemed to him most significant. For art, he said, is the natural solace of men's labour; "a solace which they once had, and always should have; the opportunity of expressing their own thoughts to their fellows by means of that very labour, by means of that daily work which nature, or long custom and second nature, does indeed require of them, but without meaning that it shall be an unrewarded or repulsive burden." The fact that the mass of men had no experience of this solace and made no demand for it appalled him who knew its value so well. He saw the poor often discontented, but it seemed to him that their discontent was ignorant, and he wished to give it knowledge. Their wages might be raised and the condition of their labour improved, but they could not therefore be happy so long as their labour itself was without joy. They must have a clear and conscious discontent with the whole commercial system, with its aim and motives, if their discontent was to produce the change that he desired; and he preached the same discontent to the middle classes and the rich. Under the present system, he told them, they too missed the happiness of art. They could not buy it with their money, for it did not exist. They could buy luxury, but that he called the supplanter and changeling of art.

> "By those who know of nothing better it has even been taken for art, the divine solace of human labour, the romance of each day's hard practice of the difficult art of living. But I say art cannot live beside it, nor self-respect in any class of life. Effeminacy and brutality are its companions on the right hand and the left."

132. **Philip Webb** (for the design) and **Morris, Marshall, Faulkner & Co.** (for the production), Table, c. 1865. Oak, 73.7 x 165 x 59.8 cm. Victoria & Albert Museum, London.

133. **Philip Webb** (for the design) and **Morris, Marshall, Faulkner & Co.** (for the production), Sideboard, c. 1862. Ebonized wood with painted and gilt decoration and panels of stamped leather; brass and copper hinges and handles, with incised decoration, 195 x 197.5 x 66 cm. Victoria & Albert Museum, London.

134. **Richard Norman Shaw,** Bookcase and Writing Desk, 1861. Cabinet. Oak, inlaid with satinwood, rosewood, walnut, bird's-eye maple and oak, partially painted, with steel hinge, 280 x 142 x 79 cm. Victoria & Albert Museum, London.

It is to be noted that Morris had no Puritan hatred of luxury and no envy of the rich man's enjoyment of it. He hated luxury because it could not be truly enjoyed and despised those living in luxury because they did not know what real pleasure was. To him it meant a waste of life for the rich as well as for the poor. It was as if men spent their time in playing a foolish game in which none of them took pleasure. The first claim he made for men was that they should have work to do that was worth doing.

"Think what a change that would make in the world! I tell you I feel dazed at the thought of the immensity of work undertaken in the making of useless things. It would be an instructive day's work for any one of us who is strong enough, to walk through two or three of the principal streets of London on a weekday, and take accurate note of everything in the shop windows which is embarrassing or superfluous to the daily life of a serious man. Nay, the most of these things no one, serious or unserious, wants at all; only a foolish habit makes even the lightest-minded of us suppose that he wants them, and to many people, even of those who buy them, they are obvious encumbrances to real work, thought and pleasure."

But it was as a workman that he looked at all this rubbish and as a workman he grew indignant when he thought of all the labour wasted upon it. "I beg you to think of the enormous mass of men who are occupied with this miserable trumpery," he cried, "men who might be occupied with work pleasant to themselves and valuable for others." For all trash must of necessity be the product of superfluous energy, and it is because we spend so much of that energy upon trash that we have so little to spare for the practice of art.

There were many people who believed, when Morris was young, that art was becoming obsolete and that man in the future would have no need of it. But Morris insisted, and the facts bore him out, that we must have art and that the only question was whether we would have it good or bad. "I must ask you to believe," he said, "that every one of the things that goes to make up the surroundings among which we live must be either beautiful or ugly, either elevating or degrading to us, either a torment and burden to the maker of it to make, or a pleasure and a solace to him." He himself looked at all the work of man's hands with the understanding of a workman, and he saw, as other men did not see, whether the maker of it had had any pleasure in making it. He brought his own new workman's test to the judgment of our society and condemned it by that test. But unlike most of those who rail at society he had his own positive notion what it should be. The value of his *News from Nowhere* lies not in his account of the process by which men attain to happiness, but in his account of that happiness when attained. In speaking of the process Morris attempted to predict without any special knowledge, but when he spoke of the happiness itself he did so with the authority of an expert. The life that he describes is in the main a life which he had led himself and which he had given up only so that he might help others to it. Thus his Utopia has superiority over most other Utopias in that we feel we should

135. **Philip Webb** (for the design) and **Morris, Marshall, Faulkner & Co.**

(for the production), Settee, c. 1865.

Oak wood with gilded gesso decoration.

Private collection.

indeed like to live in it. It may be that mankind will never be able to order their affairs so that this kind of happiness shall be shared by all, but at any rate it is a credible kind of happiness, agreeable to human nature and free from that ennui which would afflict most men in Paradise if they did not change their natures upon entering it. For in his Utopia there is not an end of labour but only labour for all men such as he himself knew and enjoyed. In a noble passage he says:

> "When all is gained that we so long for, what shall we do then? That great change that we are working for, each in his own way, will come like other changes, as a thief in the night, and will be with us before we know it; but let us imagine that it has come suddenly and dramatically, acknowledged and hailed by all right-minded people, and what shall we do then lest we begin once more to heap up fresh corruption for the woeful labour of ages once again? I say, as we turn away from the flagstaff where the new banner has been just run up, as we depart, our ears yet ringing with the blare of the heralds' trumpets that have proclaimed the new order of things, what shall we turn to then, what must we turn to then? To what else save to our work, our daily labour?"

In *News from Nowhere* the change does come suddenly and dramatically and seems to free men from most of the vices and weaknesses that express themselves in our present society. Such is the defect of the book, for we know that no change could do that, and we expect even a romance of the future to be based upon what we know about ourselves. But in the passage I have just quoted Morris shows that he does not expect this sudden and dramatic change. His real point, both here and in *News from Nowhere*, is that we have missed the path to happiness, and to a possible happiness which has been enjoyed in the past and may be enjoyed more fully in the future. We are now wandering lost, he thought, and we shall not long be content to do that. That change, of which he spoke as coming like a thief in the night, meant that men would regain their sense of direction. They would have a scent for the happiness that was possible to them when once they had found they could not be kept from it by the institutions and current ideas of the time.

He expected a vast revolution in the minds of all men such as had already happened in his own mind, and because it had happened to him he thought it might happen as quickly and consciously to others. Here, no doubt, he was mistaken. Changes such as he hoped for, changes which give a new direction to a whole society, do not happen in ten years or twenty; but they do happen. One such change occurred when the society of the ancient world began to desire a new faith more than it desired to preserve its existing civilisation. That change meant the end of the ancient world, and Morris, in his dislike of his present society, was ready to see it destroyed like that of the ancient world, if there was no other way of bringing about the change he desired. But he hoped and laboured for a revolution less long drawn and disastrous. His belief was that if men could be made to understand clearly what kind of life was desirable, they

136. Pair of High-Backed Chairs, 1856.
Victoria & Albert Museum, London.

225

would desire it strongly enough to obtain it, not without fighting perhaps, but without completely sacrificing the gains of the past. He had no blind hatred of science. Like Euripides in the *Bacchæ*, he said, "And science – we have loved her well, and followed her diligently, what will she do? I fear she is so much in the pay of the counting house and the drill sergeant, that she is too busy and will for the present do nothing." He wished to give science a new business, to make use of all that we have learnt since the Renaissance, but to make use of it so that we can obtain what we desire as a society, and not what a few rich men wish to force upon us.

"What we desire as a society." He believed that societies had desires, could be made conscious of them, and could achieve them. For that reason he was a Socialist, and for that reason he thought that the western world had taken a wrong turn at the Renaissance. For the Renaissance, with its new delight in knowledge, power and splendour, in all the possibilities which life suddenly opened to the fortunate individual, gave up the conception of a society with a common desire to be realised, that conception which made the glory of the early Middle Ages with all their imperfection of practice. With the Renaissance, in art and in life the individual triumphed and the notion prevailed that society existed to produce splendid individuals, that it was a state of war in which some men might prove the possibilities of human nature by conquering the rest. Morris himself was a splendid individual, but he had no wish to be a conqueror. He believed, indeed, that the conquerors in such a society might be splendid at first but that afterwards they would be hard and mean and little. He saw the American millionaire as the successor of the Renaissance despot, just as Domitian was the successor of Julius Caesar, and in art he saw the modern academician as the successor of Michelangelo.

"When the great masters of the Renaissance were gone, they, who, stung by the desire of doing something new, turned their mighty hands to the work of destroying the last remains of living popular art, putting in its place for a while the results of their own wonderful individuality; when these great men were dead, and lesser men of the ordinary type were masquerading in their garments, then at last it was seen what the new birth really was; then we could see that it was the fever of the strong man yearning to accomplish something before his death, not the simple hope of the child, who has long years of life and growth before him."

And as it was with art, so, he thought, it was with society. The desire of the individual, the competitive desire for predominance, is feverish, blind and unhappy. The desire of a society is a long and patient hope which the individual can share without expecting to accomplish it all himself and in his own day; and yet he can obtain happiness from his own small accomplishment. It was in art that Morris saw most clearly the proof of this. The great cathedrals of the Middle Ages were not built by the heroes of art, indeed many of them are unconnected with the name of a single artist – they were built by societies of workmen, each one of whom must have taken delight in his own little task. And Morris believed that we can build a civilisation as those workmen built a

137. Pine Table, 1856.
Pine wood.
Cheltenham Art Gallery & Museums,
Gloucestershire.

227

cathedral. To the worshipper of the strong man he, himself a strong man, would have made answer by pointing to the churches of Bourges or Chartres. If there is an activity in which the man of genius can triumph, he would have said, it is art, the activity of expression. Yet here are the greatest triumphs of art, and they are not triumphs of a single man of genius, but of a society of workmen. And they are triumphs because in them the powers of every individual were heightened by the common aim. There was not a conflict among them as to which should master the rest or take another man's work from him. Their labour meant peace, for it was done to fulfil a conception that grew in the minds of all.

Morris may never have heard of the doctrine of the Overman; but if he had heard of it we can guess what he would have thought of it. He would have seen in it a last feverish attempt to revive the glory of the Renaissance, to forget the experience of the last four hundred years, and to think as if we were once again just emerging from the failure of the later Middle Ages. That doctrine of the Overman was attempted then in art and in life, and it failed because neither the Overmen themselves nor their admirers knew 'what they wanted to do with their predominance. Power, pleasure, glory – these are only words expressing vague general conceptions. If any man takes them for an end they tell him nothing of the means by which that end can be accomplished. But that happiness of daily work which Morris knew himself and desired for all men, that is something at once precise and infinitely diverse; it is an end which suggests to every man, according to his natural bent, the means by which it may be accomplished.

Since the Renaissance, philosophers and statesmen, whatever they have devised or accomplished, have never had any clear notion of a society in which the ordinary man should make the most of his natural gifts and should attain to happiness by doing so. Even those democrats who have most ardently desired the well-being of the people have conceived for them a negative rather than a positive happiness. They have wished to give them freedom, security and good wages; and it has always seemed that they could only obtain those at the expense of the rich and powerful. Against this negative democratic ideal aristocratic philosophers like Nietzsche have raged, seeing no alternative to the predominance of the great except the dull tyranny of mediocrity. Morris believed that a society could make a third choice. He believed that all political theories of modern times had been spun in minds that had never experienced the best kind of happiness and could not, therefore, conceive of a society in which that happiness prevailed. The alternative of a splendid aristocracy and a dull democracy did not exist for him, for he himself was neither a splendid aristocrat nor a dull democrat. He was a craftsman, and the first of his kind, to consider politics as a craftsman. He saw that in the modern world the craftsman is everywhere subordinate, indeed that he was ceasing to exist, and that was the reason, he believed, why the ordinary man, robbed of his chance of creation, had become mediocre. Every man, he held, ought to be creative according to his natural powers, and, even for the ablest, to think without creating means unhappiness and intellectual error. His desire, therefore, was for a

138. **Philip Webb** (for the design) and **Morris, Marshall, Faulkner & Co.**
(for the production), Side Table.
Oak, with turned legs and strechers,
drawer with brass drop-handles,
73.6 x 167 x 60.9 cm.
Private collection.

139. **John Henry Dearle** (for the design) and **Morris & Co.** (for the production),
Screen, 1885-1910.
Glazed mahagony frame, with panels of
canvas embroidered with silks in darning,
stem and satin stitches, 162.9 x 166.2 x 2.8 cm.
Victoria & Albert Museum, London.

society in which the craftsman should be esteemed and powerful, in which the mass of men should wish to be craftsmen, and should look for happiness in the practice of some craft rather than in domination or in pleasure pursued for its own sake.

He saw no impossibility in this, for machinery has now so much increased our power of production that, if society were well organised, we should have a great deal of energy to spare after we had produced all that we could reasonably want in the way of necessaries. Indeed, as it is, we have a great deal of energy to spare, but we waste it on activities that bring no one much happiness and indeed cause want where there should be plenty. This waste has often been denounced, but Morris saw that there is no remedy for it except a change of heart in civilised mankind. Men must desire something different from what they desire; they must have new values and new standards. They must see that even the richest and most powerful of them have missed the path to happiness and missed it because they have thought rather of means rather than ends. Therefore he came forward, as an expert in happiness, to tell them what happiness was; and this, behind all his anger and denunciation, remained always his real purpose.

In the main his morality was the Christian morality, so little understood in our time, but he gave it a new application to satisfy a new want. He applied it to work, as others had applied it to conduct generally, because he saw that it had been most perverted and forgotten with regard to work. The essence of the Christian morality, and indeed of the unchanging orthodox morality of all ages, is the belief, as Morris put it in the *Dream of John Ball*, that fellowship is life and the lack of fellowship is death. It is not by competition that men are forced to do the best they can do, for that only drives them into furious and blind labours. Rivalry seems sometimes to be forced upon men by the conditions of life, but they only attain freedom when they rise above it; and to glorify this rivalry as a means of progress is to worship, like a savage, a hideous and bloodstained idol. Great men show their greatness, not by conquest but by service. There are not two races of men, the eminent and the abject, but only one race, differing among themselves in power, but all capable of some kind of excellence if all will work together in fellowship. Morris, I have said, applied this morality to work; for he believed, both from his study of past ages and from his own experience, that all men were capable of happiness and of excellence in their work if only they were not set to vain and hopeless drudgery by their masters. He saw that in all there was a spirit that could be suppressed or encouraged, and that the whole of society was made poorer by its suppression. Everywhere he saw the lack of it in the work of his own time, the work, as he said, of labour-slaves, not of free craftsmen; work which men were set to do because they were thought to be capable of nothing better, because they were regarded as cheap machines working for the profit of their masters. To him there was something sacred in all the work of men, as to the Christian there is something sacred in men themselves; and the waste of work that he saw in all the ugliness and vain luxury about him was the waste of men's lives.

140. **Morris & Co.** (for the production),
    St James, 1881.
    Wallpaper design for St James' Palace.
    Calmann & King, London.

141. *Fritillary*, 1885.
    Wallpaper design.
    Private collection.

142. *Anemone*, 1876.
    Pattern for fabric.
    Victoria & Albert Museum, London.

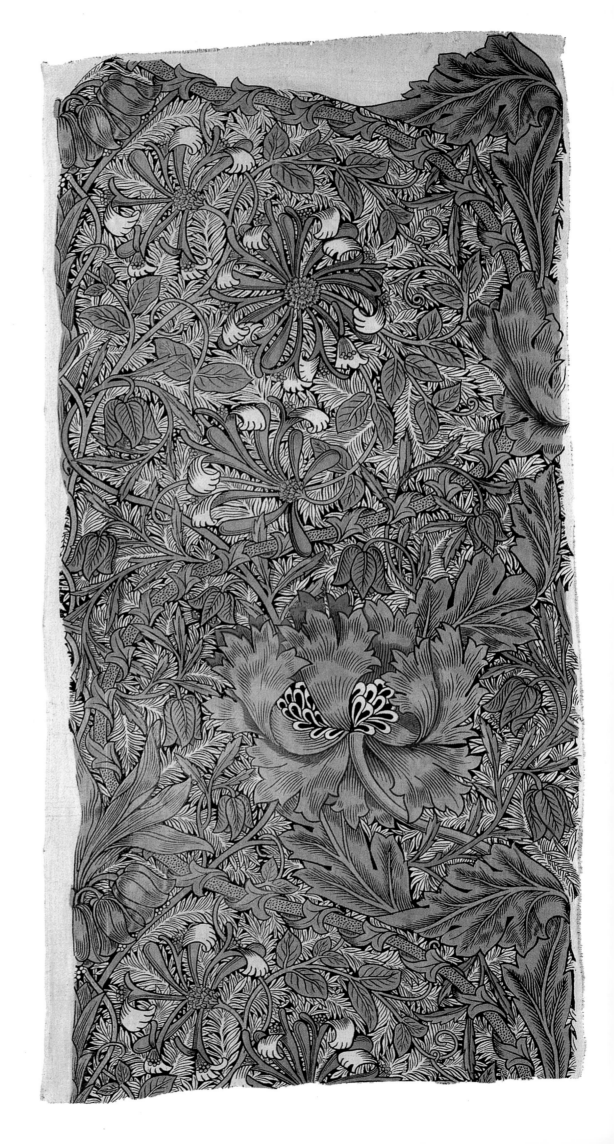

143. *Lea*, 1912.

   Block-printed cotton.

   Private collection.

144. *Honeysuckle*, 1876.

   Furnishing fabric. Block-printed silk,

   49.5 x 99 cm.

   Victoria & Albert Museum, London.

145. *Cherwell*, 1887.

   Pattern for printed velvet.

   Private collection.

Maturity and Assertion

Most of us are as indifferent to all this ugliness and vain luxury as a Roman noble of the Republic was indifferent to the slaves toiling on his land. As they were not human beings to him, so these ugly and useless things are not the work of human beings to us. They happen, and we are used to them; but Morris laboured to make us see in them symptoms of the unhappy drudgery of men as capable of doing better as we are ourselves. "If I could only persuade you of this," he said in one of his lectures, "that the chief duty of the civilised world today is to set about making labour happy for all, to do its utmost to minimise the amount of unhappy labour – nay, if I could only persuade some two or three of you here present – I should have made a good night's work of it."

"To set about making labour happy for all." That sounds a wild impossibility perhaps, but so does everything for which the heroes of the world have laboured. An American critic tells us that Morris "more than almost any other man of his age had the romantic indifference to the law of cause and effect which locks events together in a kind of static system, and the bondage of logic he never suffered." That is true of him and also of all the men that we most admire. They have believed more in the will of man and in his power to change his life than in this intimidating law of cause and effect, which locks events together in a kind of static system; and their belief has been justified by results or we should not admire them. It may not be possible to make labour happy for all; but the effort to do it will make labour a great deal less unhappy for many. For it is such an effort that changes the minds of men, making them value what they once despised and despise what they once valued. Such changes may themselves be examples of the law of cause and effect; but they would never happen unless there were men like Morris who did not suffer the bondage of logic. In fact Morris was himself an originating cause, if we care to describe him in that kind of jargon. He was something that happened and that is likely to have many important results, for he has changed the minds of many and imposed his own values, not by some spell but by an appeal to reason and commonsense. Yet this appeal, perhaps because of its very simplicity, puzzles the same clever American critic. "There is nothing immoral in Morris's work," he says, "but of morality in it we do not think at all, save as another term to distinguish the beautiful from the ugly." It would rather be true to say that for Morris beauty was another term to distinguish good from evil. He did not restrict morality but extended it. He was aware of good where others saw only beauty and of evil where others saw only ugliness. Whistler has told us that "art happens" and in saying that he was only expressing the belief of the ordinary Philistine. Morris insisted that art did not happen any more than the British Constitution happened, for to him art meant, not the work of a few men of genius but all work in which men express the pleasure of work. He himself could turn workingmen, chosen at a venture, into artists; and therefore he believed that society could do the same.

So far from having a romantic indifference to the law of cause and effect, he saw a connection of cause and effect that no one had seen before him. So far from

146. *Pink and Rose*, c. 1890.
Hand-block-printed wallpaper, 55.9 x 71.1 cm.
Private collection.

caring nothing for morality, he preached a new doctrine of morals where the world before him had seen nothing but chance beauty or chance ugliness. He himself, clear of purpose and strong of will, laboured to make the purpose of society more clear, and its will more powerful. He was a visionary but not a sentimentalist; an artist who was not hostile to science, for he did not believe that real science could be hostile or indifferent to art. Just as Leonardo da Vinci, the master of many arts, turned in the prime of the Renaissance to the new science of his time, lured by its infinite promise, so Morris, also master of many arts, turned to a new science of his own time, lured by its still more infinite promise. But the science to which he turned was one which art had taught him, for it was the science by means of which men might become conscious of, and acquire, the art of life. For him that was not an art of living beautifully, but one of making wonderful and beautiful things; and, because he himself had the power of excelling in so many crafts, it might be thought that he was not a good judge of the ordinary man's capacity for happiness. He would have said that in our present society men are forced to be ignorant of their own capacities. Some of them are specialised so that they use their brains more than is good for them; the rest are specialised so that they do not use them in their work at all.

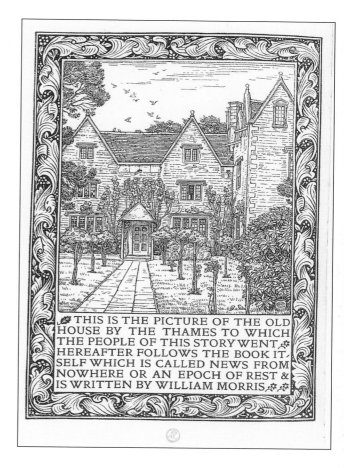

However clever we may be, talking brilliantly rather than thinking clearly, as we remain uncertain what we most value in life; Morris did not expect all men to be clever – indeed, he himself was apt to be a little frightened or suspicious of obviously clever men; but he believed that the mass of men could attain to its own kind of sagacity, its own clear sense of values, if, as individuals, they could do work exercising their hands and brains alike. And he further believed that no society could be stable, unless the majority of men attained this wisdom, unless they had profound contentment with their lives founded on contentment with their work.

There are many reformers today who think that the life of the poor ought to be brightened by amusements and excursions. Morris would never have been satisfied with such palliatives any more than with "gas and water Socialism." He wanted all men, rich and poor, to enjoy themselves in their workshops; and then, he believed, they would have no trouble in enjoying themselves outside them. Nearly all the amusements of rich and poor alike are now passive. He believed that a man must be something of an artist in his work, if he is to be anything of an artist in his play. With us the turntable has taken the place of the folk-song, but the poor would not endure turntables or any other mechanical substitute for art, if they knew what art was from their own practice of it.

Most people think of Morris as a man who tried to change the taste of his time; and, since taste is to them an arbitrary thing, Morris for them is merely the poetic upholsterer, as Lord Grimthorpe called him. He set a new fashion in patterns and furniture, which has been superseded by other fashions.

147. Kelmscott Manor.

Photograph.

© Oxfordshire, UK/The Stapleton Collection.

148. *News From Nowhere*, published in 1893.

Ink on paper, 20.5 x 14 cm.

Victoria & Albert Museum, London.

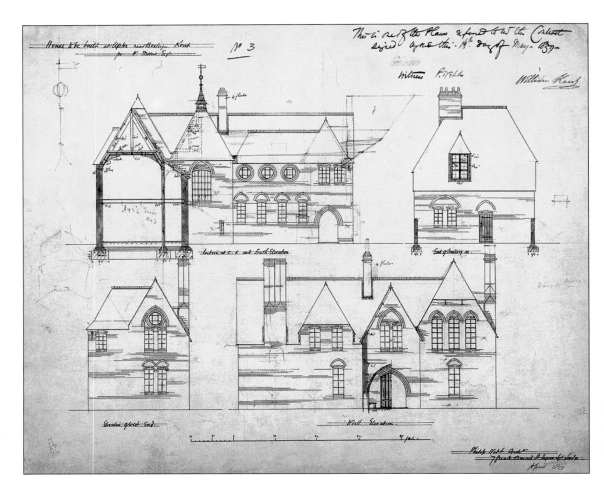

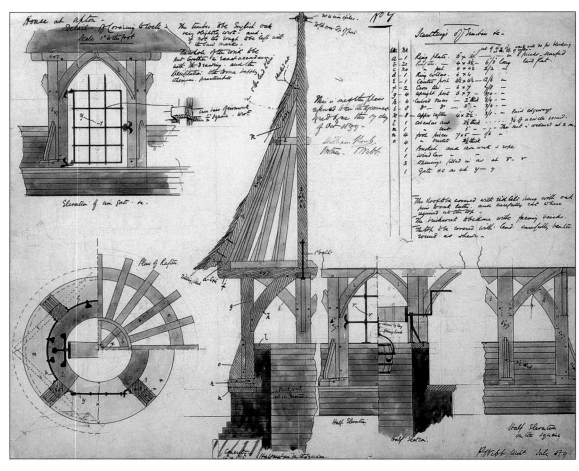

149. **Philip Webb**,
Architectural Drawing for the Red House, 1839.
North and south elevations and details,
52.1 x 63.5 cm.
Victoria & Albert Museum, London.

150. **Philip Webb**,
Architectural Drawing for the Red House, 1839.
Details of the roof over the well, 53 x 65.8 cm.
Victoria & Albert Museum, London.

151. The Red House, build in 1860.
Detail of windows on the west front.
Brexley Heath, Kent.
© NTPL/Andrew Butler.

In fact, Morris was more concerned with matters of taste than any great man before him; but that was because he saw the relation among taste and morals and reason. His effort was, not to exalt taste above everything else, but to show its connection with man's other faculties. He grew angry with the vulgarities of the art of his time, not merely because they displeased his senses, but because he, as a workman, knew what effect they must have on the workmen who produced them. And he insisted upon the importance of good taste, because he knew that those who had learnt to feel the workman behind his work could only acquire it. We know that that is true of the arts of painting, sculpture, and poetry. He insisted that it is true of everything. He worked to make us feel the workman behind everything produced by man.

Everything so fashioned cannot, of course, be art; but at present hardly anything is art, because we do not feel the workman behind his work and have no desire to sense him. To us most of man's creations are simply an uglier kind of nature. We expect in them the finish and precision of a natural process, but not its beauty. If we could acquire Morris's sense of the workman behind the work, we should not expect this finish and precision in it – indeed, we should dislike them because they hide the workman. We might accept them when unavoidable, but the pressure of our demand would be in favour of work in which the workman was not hidden, and this change of demand must inevitably produce a great change in supply. The change in taste Morris advocated cannot come without a moral change; it is not enough to like rough-looking work merely as a matter of fashion. You can do that without feeling the workman behind his work at all; and commerce will at once meet your demand with objects that are merely worse made than the old ones. What we want is not commerce doing its worst but the workman doing his best; and we must learn to regard him as a human being through his work before we can feel in that work the pleasure that he feels in putting his best into it.

That is what taste meant to Morris; and that was why he saw a new connection between the art, science, and morals of life. As the great mystics have seen the mind of God working in all natural things, so he saw the mind of man working in all things made by man; and he saw when it was working well or ill, when the work expressed the disinterested passion of the workman, and when it expressed only his employer's desire for gain. The Renaissance, with all its triumphs of art, started the decline of art and of taste, because it was then that men began to lose their sense of the workman behind his work in all the humbler arts of life and even in the great art of architecture. What Morris desired was a new Renaissance based upon a return of this sense, and he saw that, if it came, it would mean nothing less than "a reconstitution of the civilised life of mankind." Whether it will come or not is still most uncertain, but if it does come, and if it gives to society the power which the old Renaissance gave to the individual, then men will not consider the political activities of William Morris a waste.

152. The Red House, build in 1860.
     Brexley Heath, Kent.
     © NTPL/Andrew Butler.

153. The "Chèvrefeuille" Room, 1887.
     Wightwick Manor, West Midlands.
     © NTPL/Andreas von Einsiedel.

154. The Billiard Room, with *Bird* tapestry weave
curtain, *Pimpernel* wallpaper and *Lily
Kidderminster* carpet.
© NTPL/Andreas von Einsiedel.

Bibliography

BURNE-JONES, Georgiana,
Memorials of Edward Burne-Jones, New York, London, The Macmillan Company, 1904.

DRINKWATER, John,
William Morris: a Critical Study, Folcroft, Folcroft Library editions, 1969.

JACKSON, Holbrook,
William Morris, London, Jonathan Cape Ltd., 1926.

MACKAIL, John William,
The Life of William Morris, Mineola (N.Y.), Dover publications, 1995.

MORRIS, May,
William Morris: Artist, Writer, Socialist, Oxford, B. Blackwell, 1936.

NAYLOR, Gillian (ed.),
William Morris by Himself: Designs and Writings, London, Macdonald Orbis, 1988.

POULSON, Christine,
William Morris, London, The Apple press, 1989.

VALLANCE, Aymer,
William Morris, his Art, his Writings, and his Public Life, London, Studio Editions, 1986.

YOOD, James and OLDKNOW, Tina,
William Morris: Animal, Artifact, New York, Abbeville Press, 2000.

$\mathcal{L}$ist of $\mathcal{I}$llustrations

Tapestry Design and Wallpaper

Tiles